FOLKLORE HISTORY SERIES

WITCHCRAFT AND WITCHCRAFT TRAILS IN ORKNEY AND SHETLAND

G. F. BLACK

British Library Cataloguing-in-Publication Data
A catalogue record for this book is available from
the British Library

CONTENTS:

WITCHCRAFT.

Orkney. The belief in witchcraft still prevails here, as in other parts of the kingdom. The character of Norna, in the Pirate, was drawn from a living original in Orkney. The old sibyl is indebted, for the fame which she has acquired, to a visit from the great Novelist, when he arrived at Stromness, where she then dwelt. She has since removed her residence to one of the smaller isles. It has been her custom to sell to the whalers charms of various kinds, as preservatives from the winds, during their arduous voyages. . . . She has given, it is said, at various times, indubitable proofs of supernatural power: on one occasion, having discovered that she had just been robbed of some geese by the crew of a brig, she anticipated its exit from the Sound by speedily crossing the hill, and taking up her position on the brow of a beetling cliff, denounced, by all her gods, the ill-fated bark to destruction. The sea instantly opened and swallowed up its victim. On another occasion, she had received some offence from a young fisherman, and predicted that ere a year had passed away his body should lie lifeless on the beach: the prognostication was fully verified.

TEIGNMOUTH, vol. i. pp. 286, 287.

Shetland. Witchcraft is still believed by the peasantry to exist in Zetland; and some old women live by pretending to be witches, for no one ventures to refuse what they ask. About six years ago [c. 1802] a man entered a prosecution in the sheriff-court at Lerwick, against a woman for witchcraft. He stated that she uniformly assumed the form of a raven, and in that character killed his cattle, and prevented the milk of his cows from yielding butter. The late Mr. Scott, then sheriff-substitute, permitted the case to come into court, and was at great pains to explain the folly and even criminality of such proceedings.   —EDMONDSTON, Shetland, vol. ii. p. 74.

Orkney. Formula of old used in Orkney to acquire witchcraft.—Mr. Dennison wrote it down nearly 50 years ago from the recital of an old Orkney woman—granddaughter of a noted witch. The formula to be gone through to obtain witchcraft (or, as Mr. Dennison says, in plain English, a formula for giving one's self to the Devil) was as follows:—

The person wishing to acquire the witch's knowledge must go to the sea-shore at midnight, must, as he goes, turn three times against the course of the sun, must lie down flat on his back with his head to the south, and on ground between the lines of high and low water. He must grasp a stone in each hand, have a stone at the side of each foot, a stone at his head, a flat stone on his chest, and another over his heart; and must lie with arms and legs stretched out. He will then shut his eyes, and slowly repeat the following Incantation:—

> O, Mester King o' a' that's ill,
> Come fill me wi' the warlock skill,

An' I sall serve wi' all me will.
Trow tak' me gin I sinno!
Trow tak' me gin I winno!
Trow tak' me whin I cinno!
Come tak' me noo, an' tak' me a',
Tak' lights an' liver, pluck an' ga',
Tak' me, tak' me, noo, I say,
Fae de how o' de head tae de tip of de tae;
Tak' a' dat's oot an' in o' me,
Tak' hide an' hair an' a' tae thee,
Tak' hert an' hams, flesh, bleud, an' büns,
Tak' a' atween de seeven stüns
I de name o' de muckle black Wallawa!

The person must lie quiet for a little time after repeating the Incantation. Then opening his eyes, he should turn on his left side, arise and fling the stones used in the operation into the sea. Each stone must be flung singly; and with the throwing of each a certain malediction was said. Mr. Dennison's inform-ant professed to have forgotten the terms of the malediction, but he rather suspected she considered the imprecations too shocking to repeat. 　　　　　　　　　　　　MACKENZIE, p. 4.

Shetland. How Women could become Witches.—When it is full moon and midnight the aspirant after unhallowed power goes alone to the sea-shore and lies down upon the beach below the flood-tide mark. She then puts her left hand under the soles of her feet and the right hand on the top of her head and repeats three times, "The muckle maister Deil tak' what's atween dis twa haunds." The devil then appears and clenches the bargain with shaking of hands. When this is done there is

no retracting. The woman is his slave, and he gives her power
on land and sea.　　　　—EDMONSTON and SAXBY, p. 206.

Witch Metarmorphosis.—I was told once of a witch who had
taught her daughter some "tricks of the trade," and the girl,
proud of her knowledge, changed herself into a raven, according to the maternal directions. But in learning how to become a bird, the girl had forgotten to receive the instructions
necessary for returning to mortal mould, and would have remained a raven if her mother had not guessed somehow the
state of the case. With great difficulty the witch contrived to
restore her daughter's personal appearance, but not all her art
could bring back the girl's natural voice. Croak she would,
and croak she could, and all her descendants after her; and
that was how the peculiar sound (called corbieing in Shetland) known as "a burr" came. EDMONSTON and SAXBY,
p. 221.

[A] witch, desirous of injuring a neighbour changed herself into a black dog, and made her way into the neighbour's
ben-end-o'-the-hoose, where she would certainly have cre-
ated serious disturbance if an old man in the family had not
recognised her by a peculiar formation of the eyelids, which,
it seems, she could not discard from her canine appearance.
Seizing the tongs, the worthy patriarch brought them down
upon the black dog's back with might and main. "Tak' doo
yon, Minnie Merran" (the witch's name), he cried, "an bear
doo da weight o' dis auld airm as lang as doo leeves."

The dog ran howling and limping out of the house, and when
next the witch was seen, she who hitherto had walked upright

and with the dignity of a Norna, leant upon a stick, and had a hump upon her back. She said she had fallen from a height, and was afraid her spine was broken; but folk called it "the mark o' auld Jockie's taings." EDMONSTON and SAXBY, pp. 221, 222.

Da Witch's Fee.—In the parish of Whiteness a man's wife was once lying very ill. Everything had been done to cure her, but she had got no better, and at last her husband thought that he would ask an old woman, who had a name for being able to do curious things with the assistance of the "trows," to come and see her. He went to the witch's cottage and explained his errand.

"Yae, my lamb, I'se come," said the old woman. "Gang du haem; I'se no be lang ahin' dee." The man returned home. As he was going up the "gaet" or footpath to his cottage door he looked behind him, but he could see nothing of the witch. Just as he was about to lift the latch he heard quick footsteps near him, and, turning round, he saw the old crone standing by his side. She laughed and said:

"Lift du da snek, and lat me look at Keetie." They went into the house and the old woman walked up close to the bed in which the sick wife lay and looked at her. Then she turned to the man and said:

"Yae, I can set her ipo fit again, but what haes du ta gie?' There happened to be in the house at the time an old silly kind of man who used to wander about, begging among the neighbours.

9

"I kno no," replied the husband, "excep du taks da auld man at's i' da but-room yundru at da fire."

"Kettie sail be able ta geng furt an mylk da kye afore da ouk is oot," said the old witch, and she went out. Next morning the old wandering man was found dead on the hillside not far from the cottage, and from that time the wife got quickly better. —BURGESS, p. 99.

Tingwall. "Luggie" the Witch.—About a Mile from Tingwal to the North, there is a Hill called the Knop of Kebister, or Luggie's Know, nigh to which Hil there is a House called Kebister, where a Varlet or Wizard lived, commonly designed Luggie, concerning whom it was reported that when the Sea was so Tempestuous, that the Boats durst not go off to the Fishing, he used to go to that Hill or Know, wherein a hole, into which he let down his Lines and took up any Fish he pleased, as a Cod or Ling, &c., which no other could do but himself: Also when Fishing at Sea, he would at his pleasure take up any rosted Fish with his Line, with the Intrals or Guts out of it, and so ready for his use: This was certainly done by the Agency of evil Spirits, with whom he was in Compact and Covenant. He being convicted of Witchcraft was burnt nigh to Scalloway. —BRAND, pp. 110, 111.
Cf. SINCLAIR, pp. 237-8.

TRIALS.

Orkney. Trial of Katherine Caray, June, 1616.—An alleged Satanic precept was, to make "a wresting thread, and give it in the name of the Father, Sone, and the Holie Gaist, and say,

Bone to bone, synnew to synnew, and flesche to flesche, and bluid to bluid, it wald mak ony wrest of man or beast haill."
                                        —DALYELL, p. 118.

In her trial it is mentioned that earth taken from the spot where a man had been slain, was prescribed for a hurt or an ulcer.   —*Ibid.*, p. 126.

When she wandered among the hills "at the doun going of the sun, ane great number of fairie men mett her "together with" a maister man."   —*Ibid.*, p. 536.

Trial of Thomas Cors, 6 April, 1643.—Being full of displeasure with James Paplay, he predictively "brust furth in thes speiches, 'thow art now the highest man that ever thow salt be! Thow ar going to shear thy corne, but it sail never doe yow good! Thow art going to sett hous with thy wyff—ye sail have no joy on of on vther: Yle sail not keip yow and hir, ye sall have such ane meit-will and sall have nothing to eat, but be fain to eat grass vnder the stanes and wair vnder the bankis,'" His neighbours not only confirmed the utterance of these predictions, but that they came to pass.   —Ibid., pp. 492-93.

Trial of Marable Couper, 1624.—I. In the first, ye, the said Marable Couper, ar indytit and accusit for airt and pairt of the vseing, comitting, and practising of the divelish and abominable cryme of Superstitioun, Witchcraft, and Sorcerie, in that, at Mid-somer, four yeiris syne or thairby, Dauid Mowat in Bankis in Birsay, haveing mareit Margaret Corstoun, they haid thrie new callowit kyne, quhairof the said Margaret wantit the proffeit; and suspecting yow, scho came to yow and reprovit yow, calling, Banisched witche, quhy had ye tane the proffeit of hir kyne; quha ansuerit hir, that it sould be sevin yeiris or ony witche tuik the proffeit agane from hir kyne. Quhairvpoun follow the nixt yeir, the said Dauid and Margaret had thrie kyne, quhairof the ane deit in callow-ing, and the calff tane out of hir wombe; the nixt callowit ane calff, and never gave milk; and the thrid thir four yeiris past never tuik bull: And at the Candlemes efter, the said Margaret meiting with yow at your awin dore, and efter many wordis and flytting, the said Margaret haueing strucken yow ffor the lose that scho had of hir kyne, ye said to hir, that by the lose of hir kyne scho sould want worth the best horse that was in Birsay: And at the Beltane thairefter, scho had ane kow that deit, and tua young beastis. Quhilk ye did not onlie be your witchcraft and divelrie, bot gave yourselff furth to haue skill to do thingis.

II. Immediatlie efter the tyme forsaid, the said Dauid Mowat, haueing met yow cuming to your hous with ane stoup of aill, quhairof ye causit him to drink; and that same night efter, he contractit seiknes, and fyftene dayis thair efter ye came to visite him, quha said, ye wald lay yourlyff for him, and that he wald ly yit ane moneth seik or he war heall; quha contin-wit seik, according to your speiche, and never slipit, and at the sext oulkis end he became heall, be your witchcraft and divelrie.

III. In harvest four yeiris syne or thairby, quhen the said Dauid first gaid to his barne with his new corne, ye cam to his hous, and quhen he gaed to the kill ye came agane, and quhen the said Margaret was grinding ane lock of beir on the quernis, ye came to the hous and said ye was come to get your kiltreis that he had borrowit; and he, haveing borrowit nane, was werrie angrie, and said he was euer cumerit with yow, and thoucht to have dung yow; and quhen he saw yow, he had no power to ding yow; bot reprowit yow, flet with yow, and bad yow away; quha gaid away: Bot efter, beith the said Margaret and hir servand could not gar the quernis gang about, and the thing that was ground was lyk dirt; and going to the mylne with the rest, it was lyk dirt as the vther: And James Spens your gud brother, being servant with them, and thay geving yow the wyte, he cam to yow and reprovit yow, and incontinentlie the rest of the meill was asse gud and fair as could be possible, be your witchcraft and divelrie.

IV. Vpoun Monday befor Fastingis evin thairefter, ye came to the said Dauid his hous, and efter mony wordis and flytting, he gaue yow ane cuff, and pat yow to the dore, and ye suore that he sould repent that straik; and four dayis efter he haueing put sex meillis of aittis vpoun his kill to dry, the kill tuik fyre and brunt, and the cornes that he got saiff he tuik to Alexander Ingsayis kill, quhilk lykwayis tuik fyre and brunt, be your witchcraft and divelrie.

V. At Alhallowmes thrie yeiris syne, the said Margaret Corstoun haueing contractit seiknes dwyned be space of foure monethis, and could get no mendis at hame, nor quhen scho wes brocht to the toun of Kirkwall; and sua returning hame againe, and going to Alexander Philipis hous by your hous, ye was standing at your dore, and the said Margaret ending in wordis and flytting with yow, called yow ane banished witche, and said giff scho deid, scho sould lay hir dead vpoun yow;

and ye said to hir, scho micht haue reprowit yow quyetlie giff scho had ony thing to say to yow; and ye tuik hir in to your hous, and tuik ane birstane stane and pat it in the fyre, and hate ane drink of ale with it, and gave hir to drink; quhairby as be your witchcraft and divelry, ye cast the seiknes, so be the lyk divelrie and witchcraft scho gat hir health.

VI. [Once] the said Margaret Corstoun cuming to your hous efter Alexander Philipis wyff and ye discordit, and being in your bed, ye layed by the lap of the claithes, and lut hir sie besyd yow, as it haid been ane great bag lyk ane swynes bledder, great at the ane end and small at the vther, quhilk ye said was your guttis that Alexander Philipis wyff had tramped out with hir knees; and that same day Oliuer Garacoat hauing cum to sumond yow to compeir befor the sessioun, ye said to him, how could ye cum, for Alexander Philipis wyff had pussit out your guttis, and butte him sie as it had bene your guttis lying besyde yow, most fearfull to look to, and was nothing bot divelrie.

VII. . . . Vpoun Monday efter Sanct Magnus day, in Boir, Imvjc [1600] and tuentie tua yeiris, Thomas Seatter, in Seatter, haveing enterit his pleuche to the beir seid, and Margaret Bimbister, his seruant, leading the pleuche, the said Margaret luked about and sawe ane cuming vp the burne, and ane blak bruch about hir, quha said to hir maister, I sie ane woman cuming vp the burne, and ane black bruche about hir, and quhen he saw hir, he beseached him to God, and said, it wes Marable Couper; and quhen scho came to the pleuche, scho said hir erand was to lay hir culter, bot scho haid nane with hir, and he bad hir send hir husband or sone, and thet urne sould be done. So ye depairting, gaid to his hous, and ane kow being callowing, ane pair of scheittis stentit about hir that scho sould not be sene, and Elspeth Thomesone, spous to the said Thomas, being besyd hir, or euer scho wist, ye was within the scheittis and luiking ouer her shoulder; quhairat, scho being affrayed, and beseaching hir to God, scho comandit yow away, and ye going furth, enterit in hir byre, and doun betuix tua kyne, and quhen ye was persawit be ane bairne, and the said Elspeth advertised thairoff, scho came furth to yow, and said it was for na gud ye was cum thair; and ye ansuerit hir, ye was cum to advertise hir that hir gudman was wattit on for his lyff, and hir kyne for evill, and that scho wald want hir kyne or hir gudman want his lyff; and schew hir that ye haid brocht ane sort of grass to saue hir kyne; and the said Elspeth being affrayed, gaid to hir gudman, and tald him, quha came hame with hir, and gart yow deliuer the grasse to his wyff, quha draiked it in leauen, and gaue it to tua dogis, quha ran wood, and ane of thame mad the forme of ryding, ane kow, quha, efter he tuiched hir with his feit, scho pisched blud, and schortlie efter raged to dead; and quhen he was put from the kow, he vsit the Iyk to four calffis, quha pisched blud lykwayis, and ceassit not quhilk he was stickit; and the vther dog lykwayis raged quhill he was libed: And within tuentie four houris efter the said kow was dead, ye came bak agane to Seatter, as it war lamenting for the dead of the kow, and said to the said Elspeth, giff scho wald let yow sie the place quhair the kow deid ye wald tell hir quhidder they war deid or liveing, that had the wyte of the kowis death.

VIII. . . . Ye gaue ane peice bannock to vmquhile Katherine Fulsetter, spous to Jon Crowdan, quha immediatly efter tuik seiknes and dwyned ane lang tyme, and ye cuming to visite her, desyrit almous of hir, and said scho wald be weill, quha gaue yow ane pynt of aill; and ye, setting the aill besyd yow, ane swyne came and cust it downe: than ye desyrit ane vther pynt of aill, quhilk scho refussit, and ye being angrie, gaid furth at the dore, and said scho sould neuer sell aill again; quhilk came to pas be your witchcraft and divelrie, for schortlie the said Katherine deid.

IX. The said Elspeth Thomesone came to your hous to seik barme, ye being sitting at the fyre syde, ye gave baith aill and barme to the divell, that was in your hous; and quhen scho reprowit yow, and said that ye haid baith aill and barme, ye sat downe vpoun your knees, and prayed to God that your soull might newer sie the kingdome of hewen, giff ye haid ayther barme or aill; bot the said Elspeth going in your seller, quhilk was dungeon mirk, and putting furth hir hand to greap about hir, hir hand chanced in ane barrell of aill with ane hat of barme vpoun it, quhilk scho teasted to be aill; and the hous growing sumquhat lighter, scho luked about hir, and saw ane halff barrell of new aill standing on ane chest head: And at the Alhallowmes efter, scho reproveand yow for your baning and swearing, and that ye sould have gevin your selff so to the devill, ye said ye haid nothing to do with the devill; bot quhen ye lay in gissing of your sone Robie, your companie came and tuk you away, and that thay fetche yow, and ye ar with thame ewerie mone anse.

X. And generallie, ye, the said Marable Couper, ar indyttit and accusit as ane comoun witche, for airt and pairt vseing, comitting, and practising of the abominable cryme of Superstition, Witchcraft, and Sorcerie, and in going with the divell, quhom ye confest takis yow away ilk mone anes; and, in geving your selff furth to haue sic constand knawledge; thairthrow abuseing the people, and wronging and slaying man and beast, and sua not onlie reput and haldin ane comoun and notorious witche, bot being convict in ane Justice Court of befor, in certane pointis of witchcraft, ye was adjudgit to be banishit the parochin of Birsay of your awin consent, and not to be sene nor found within it, vnder the paine of taking the cryme of witchcraft vpoun yow: And thairfor, and seing ye have maid your continwalle residence in the said parochin sensyne, ye aucht and sould of new agane vndergo the tryall of ane assyse, and be adjudgit and condemnit to the death, for the caussis forsaid, and in example of vtheris to do the lyk; and your guidis and gear to be escheit and inbrocht to his Majesteis vse, conforme to the lawis and daylie practique observit in sic caissis.

Curia Justiciariae vicecomitatus de Orkney, tenta apud Kirkwall, septimo die mensis July, per Dominum Joannem Buchannane, anno Domini 1624.

[She was found guilty of most of the charges before the assize.]

Sentence.

The Judge acceptis the determinatioun of the Assyse, and ordainis the pannell to be tane be the lockman, hir hands bund, and be caried to the head of the Lon, the place of execution, and thair to be knet to ane staik, wiried to the death, and brunt in asses. Quhilk Donald Kenner, dempster, gave for dome.

Abbotsford Club Miscellany, vol. i. pp. 135-142.

Trial of Katherine Cragie, alias Estquoy, 1640.—Ye, the said Katherein ar indyted and accusit for . . . vsing and practising of Witchcraftis, Sorceries, and Divinatiouns, and in gevin your sel furth to haue sick craft and knowledge, and in companie and societie with the devill, and thair-throw abusand the people. . . .

I. In speciall . . . in comeing to Jonet Cragie, spouse to Robert Robsone, alias Costas, hir hous, the said Robert Robsone being deadlie seik, and non that evir cam to visit him expected that he could recover from that sicknesse; ye cam to hir hous befor daylight, and spak to him (who at that time knew nothing that wes done or spoken besyd him for heavie sicknesse) on this maner: "What now, Robbie, ar ye going to die? I grant that I prayed ill for you, and now I sie that prayer hath taken effect": And leiving of farder speaking to him, ye said to the said Jonet Cragie on this maner: "Jonet, if I durst trust in you, I sould know quhat lyeth on your guidman, and holdis him doun at the grund; I suld tell whether it wer ane hill-spirit, a kirk-spirit, or a water-spirit, that so troubles him." The said Jonet Cragie ansuerit yow again, schoe sould nevir reveall any thing vpon yow, if ye helped hir guidman. Whairupon ye replyed to hir, "Well, or the morne at evin I sail witte whether it be a hill-spirit, a kirk-spirit, or a water-spirit, that troubles him." The nixt morne thairefter, [ye] the said Katharein cum to the said Jonet's house befor day, and brocht with yow thrie stones, which ye put on the fyre, wher they continowed all the day till eftir sone sette; and than ye took thame out of the fyre, laying thame vnder the threshold of the doore, where they continowed all night till vpon the morrow timeous befor sun rysing, ye took thame vp frome vnder the said doore threshold, and taking a veshell filled with water, ye put the stones thairin severallie, on after another; of which stones, being thus put into the said water be yow, the said Jonet Cragie hard on of thame chirme and churle into the water, wharvpon ye said to the said Jonet on this maner: "Jonet, it is a kirk-spirit which troubleth Robbie your husband." Thairefter ye gave the vessel with the water to the said Jonet, whairunto ye haid put the thrie stones, and directed her to wasch hir husband thairwith.

II. Item, for putting of vther thrie stones into the fyre, quhair they continowed all the day also, till sunsette, at which tyme ye did tak them out, and layed thame again vnder the threshold of the dure, quhar thay continowed all that night, till vpon the morn tymeouslie, befor sun rysing, ye did again tak vp the said thrie stones from vnder the said doore threshold, and did tak a veshell, as ye did the day before, filled with water, wherein again ye put the thrie stones severallie, on after another, of which forsaid stones, being thus put in the water be you, the said Jonet hard thame again, the secund tyme, chirme and churle into the water; and thairefter gave hir the said vessell with the water, and causit her wasch hir husband with it a secund tyme.

III. Item, ye ar indyted and accusit . . . the thrid tyme, in takin the stones and putting thame vnder the threshold of the doore all that night, and in the vessell with the water vpon the morning therafter, as was done before, and one of the stones chirmed and churled in the water, as twyce before it had done, but wold not geve the said Jonet the vessell with the water to wasch hir husband, as scho haid done befor at your directioun, but ye did wasch him with the water your self.

IV. Item, ye ar indyted and accusit for the devilrie committit be yow in comeing to the said Jonet Cragie's hous, ye haring tell that scho had revealled these proceidingis of yours vsit upon the said Robert Robbesone hir husband; scho not being at home, and missing her, ye said to on of her children on this maner (as the child reported and as it fell out accordinglie), "Thy mother hes bein tailing tealls of me, but I sall put a buckie in her scheek for that, that all her kinne sall never get out: So it cam to passe that thair grew a great byle vpon the said Jonet's left cheek, which disfigured her face, by drawing her mouth vp to hir right eare, as is manifest: Wharvpon the said Jonet, finding hir self thus tormented, scho sent for yow, and reproved yow, and said to yow that ye had witched hir; ye answered hir again, that it was but the Trow that haid gripped her; and vpon the nixt day thairefter, ye cam to the said Jonetis hous befor day, and brought with yow the Trowis gloue, and folded the same about the said Jonet's craige thrie several tymes, and vpol the thrid day the byle brak; but, as all people may sie, the said Jonet's mouth is not as it was wont to be.

V. Item, ye ar indyted and accusit for . . . comeing to James Traill, he being labouring his land, with a vessel full of water in your hand, which ye offered him, desyring him to ressave it from yow, and to cast the same water amongst his bear-seed, promising to him, if he wold doe that according to your directioun, he sould thairby get a good crope of cornes.

VI. Item, ye ar indyted and accusit . . . for comeing to Issobell Cragie, relict of umquhile George Traili of Wesnesse; he and the said Issobell being privatlie together, and non with you in the hous of Wesnesse, ye spak to the said Issobell, saying, "Tell me if ye have a mynd to haue Harie Bellendeyne to be your husband, and, if yow please, I will geve yow a grasse which, being vsit at my directioun, it will caus Harie Bellenden never to haue ane other woman but your self."

VII. Item, ye ar indyted and accusit for . . . going to Jonet Sclaitter's hous, William Flais, in Crage, her husband, being lyand seik, and said to her, "Jonet, if ye wold haue your husband ressaue some littill heillth (for he will never recover of that seiknes quhilk he is lying in), ye sail go with me about the Crosse Kirk of Wesbuster, and the Locke of Wesbuster, befor sun rysing," and desyrit hir to keip silence and not to speak a word.

The Judge absolvis the pannell.
Abbotsford Club Miscellany, v. i. pp. 164-169.

Second Trial of Katherine Cragie, 1643.—Ye the said Katherine Cragie, alias Estayuoy, are indytit and accusit . . .

I. In speciall, in that . . . [in] . . . March 1642 yeiris, James Caithnes in Rowsay, having gone over to Westray for doing sum of his effairis thair, and culd not get home tymeouslie to his hous, for ill weather; in the meantyme, quhill his wyif was thinking long for hir husbandis home-cumming, ye cam to hir, and said to hir, "Give me ane peice of cloath, als much as will be ane pair of handshouse, and your husband sall get fair weather to come home shortlie, before ye get your supper"; and vpoun the morne, the weather becam fair and the said James cam home.

II. Ye ar indytit and accusit that Thomas Corse being lying deadlie seik, and in all menis judgment quha saw him without hop to live langer, and being for the tyme sensles, not knowe-ing quhat was done or said to him, ye cam to his hous, and said to Margaret Craigie, his wyif, that the said Thomas wold not die of that seiknes; and ye assurit hir thairof, and ye bro-cht with yow thrie stanes to the hous, quhilkis tymous in the morneing, ye laid in thrie corneris or nookis of the hearth, quher the samen continwit till about day-setting; and then ye did, with your awin handis tak vp the thrie stones from their severall places, and laid thame behind the dore all night; and tymous in the morneing, ye did tak vp these thrie cold stones, and put thame in ane vessell, with water, when the said Mar-garet hard on of these stones chirme and churle in the water, but as yit ye told her not quhat spirit trublit hir husband. Eft-erward ye cam with the water, and washed the said Thomas Corse thairwith, at quhilk tyme he was so sensles that he knew not quhat was done to him: efter as ye haid waschen him the first tyme, ye again took the thrie stanes, and vsit thame the secund and thrid tyme, as at the first, and washed him with the water, as at the first; and quhill ye war wasching him the thrid tyme, he bame somquhat sensible, and knew that ye war wasching him, quhich he perceavit not the two former tymes ye did wash him. And immediatlie the same

day, tymeous in the morning, efter as ye haid washen him
the thrid tyme, ye desyrit the said Margaret Craigie his wyif
to goe about the loch with yow for getting of hir husbandis
health; but the said Thomas Corse begining at the same tyme
to recover and to becom sensible, hearing your speich to his
wyif, stayit hir, that shoe went not with yow.

III. Item, ye ar indytit and accusit . . . in that . . . Thomas
Irwing, younger, being verie seik in Quondale, quhairfra he
was flitting, he was brocht in to Jonet Sklateris hous in Cog-
are, heavilie diseasit with a senslesnes, that he knew not quhat
was said or done to him; ye cam to the said Jonet Sklateris
hous, and knoweing that the said Thomas was lying seik in
his hous, ye said that it was the sea trow or spirit that was lying vpoun him, which might weill enuch be flyed away, and
efter this, ye went and brocht with yow thrie stones, and laid
thame in thrie corneris or nooks of the hearth, from morneing till night, then ye took thame vp in your hand, and laid
thame behind the dore all night till tymous in the morneing;
at which tyme, ye took vp the thrie cold stones and put thame
severallie into a weschell with water, quhair the said Jonet
hard on of the stones chirme and churle. Thairefter, ye took
the water and washed the said Thomas thairwith; but he was
so sensles that he knew not that ye haid washen him. This ye
did with the stones and water thrie several] tymes and morn-
ingis togither to him, and efter, as ye haid washen him the
thrid tym, immediatlie that same night following ye causit
him to ryse out of his bed vndir silence and cloud of night,
to go with yow to the sea schore, forbidding him to speak
at all, be the way, till your returne to the hous of Cogar, and
so ye went befoir, and the said Thomas followit yow, and be

the way he was sore affrayed and many tymes thocht not to haue gone further with yow; but ye speaking nothing only beakned to him with your hand to goe fordward with yow to the appoyntit place. So ye went with the said Thomas doun beneath the bridge of Savaskaill, at the sea schore, wher ye did tak thrie looffull of water, and did cast the samin ower his head, and after-wardis he returnit with yow to the hous of Cogar, befoir any of the house war risen out of thair beddis; and everie day thairefter he convalescit and becam better of his seiknes.

IV. Item, ye ar indytit and accusit, that . . . ye being in Margaret Craigies hous, the said Margaret haid ane young quoyak calfe, whilk did eat ane beat of lint vnto yow, quhairvpoun, ye being verie angrie, said to the said Margaret, "ye sall nevir milk hir; dogis sail eat hir. Knowe ye not quhat becam of Rowie Flawis kow, quhilk did eat my courtch?" (for it was of treuth, that efter the kow had eattin your curch, shoe nevir did moir good). Efter these your wordis, the calfe becam a beast of thrie yieris auld, went to the hill quhair it died, was nevir found till the doggis haid eattin.

V. Item, ye ar indytit and accusit, That vpoun ane Saturday in winter, . . . when William Flawis in Cogar was lying seik, ye cam to Henrie Yorstounes hous, and lodgit thair all night, and arose tymous in the morneing, being Sunday, a litle befoir the break of day, being verie tempestuous weather with snow and sleit, the said Henrie and Katherin Windwik his spous, and thair children, being all as yet in thair beddis, ye sought ane garter from ane of the bairnes, but they vnwilling to ryse, refusit yow: As ye wer going out of the hous, ye wold haue haid ane of the bairnes to haue steikit the dore efter yow, but the bairnes vnwilling to ryse, desyrit yow to draw to the samen efter yow, quhilk ye wold not doe. Vpoun Monday, in the morneing, the said Katherin Windwik went to Thomas Corse his hous to visit him, thinking that he was eather dead or verie neir, and non that haid sein him the night befor thoght that he culd escap, and quhen shoe cam in to his hous, sieing the said Thomas lying in his bed laughing, and yow sitting in the hous, steppit in by, to goe neir to Thomas Corse, quhair he lay, and in the bygoing, ye spak quyetlie to hir in hir ear on this maner, "quhat sikane morneing, think ye, haid I yesterday?" quha ansuerit yow, "quhy, quhat glangoir war ye doing in that ill weather?" Ye said to hir againe, "I was about the loch with Jonet Sklateris, spous to William Flawis, but it is for no stead, it will never mend hir." These thingis began to be rumorit, and the sessioun being acquantit thairwith, the said vmquhile Henrie Yorstoun was cited, and declarit the samen done by yow, and told to him be his wyif. After- wardis, ye being lodging in Essen Corse his hous, short efter, ye said "Henrie Yorstoun hes bein making reportis of me, but er ane yeir be at ane end he sall find it"; and so it fell out, that the said Henrie Yorstoun contracted great seiknes, and died within the yeir efter, as ye haid wented your anger againest him, and efter the death of the said Henrie Yorstoun, the said Essen Corse told the said Katherine Windwik your irefull wordis vttered againest hir said vmquhile husband; and this also cumming to the knowledge of the sessioun, and being cited to declair quhat he knew thairin; but er the sessioun day came, the said Essen, taking with him his sone, ane yong boy to the craiges to draw fish, but the said Essen Corse was takin out with ane swelling sea and drowned, and the chyld

25

escaped: Quhilk was done be your witchcraft and devilrie.

VI. Item, . . . quhen William Flawis in Cogar was lyand seik, ye took Jonet Sklatter, his wyif, and Margaret Irwing, his servant woman, with yow, quhair ye direct the said Jonet to follow yow, and causit the said Margaret Irwing follow the said Jonet, and went about the loch in this ordour, and about the four nookis of the kirk yaird, and none of yow spak ane word all the while, quhair in your progress and regress, ye returnit in that same maner, ye the said Katherin going still befoir. At last, cumming to the hous, ye enterit in the hous first, and steppit into the seller quhair the said William Flawis was lying seik, and the said Jonet Sklatter and her woman followit yow, and quhen ye and they enterit in the seller, ye than began to speak, and bad the said Margaret lay her hand in William Flawis' hand, quhair he was lying, quhairat the said Margaret began to fear some mischief intendit against hir, and was verie loth to do it; yit, at last, shoe took him by the hand verie slenderlie; this done, ye bad the said Margaret gang but the hous, quhairat the said Margaret became ver-ie fearit, and weipit, and sat doun, and wold onowayis stirr, nor goe first out. Thairfoir, ye went out first your selff; and quhen the lass cam but the hous, ye began to flyt with hir becaus shoe wold not goe first out. After these thingis, vpoun ane vther day, quhen the said Margaret haid come in from hir work, the said Williame being lying seik, shoe fand yow standing vpoun the floore, holding something close betuix your handis, and ye cam to hir, and held the samen to hir left ear, and said to hir, hearest thow that? and the said Margaret hard sumthing chaking werie quyetlie at hir ear, then shoe askit yow quhat it was shoe hard; and ye ansuerit, it was ane stane which was clowen, and water haid enterit in betuix both halfis of it, and it was the water that pized within the stone.

VII. Item, . . . ye being dwelling with Thomas Corse wyf, Margaret Craigie said, if it happint yow to be out of the house in the farthest pairt of the yle, all that shoe wold speak in hir awin house, most secretlie and privatlie, ye at your first home cumming to the hous, ye wold tell her of it: Quhilk revelatioun and foirknowledge ye haid of the devill, your maister.

VIII. Item, . . . quhen ye dwelt with Katherin Windwik, spous to Gilbert Mowat, if it had chanched yow to have bein furth at work, or haid bein in the farthest pairt of the yle, though shoe suld even [do] a thing nevir so secretlie, and it had bein but to heat a drink to her self quyetlie, quhairof shoe thought thair was none that culd have knowledge, yet, quhen ye cam home ye wold tell her of it: Quhilk revelatioun and foirknoweledge ye haid of the devill, your maister.

IX. Item, . . . quhen Magnus Harcas was tormentit with ane intollerable paine in his leg, ye cam to him quhair he was lying, and desyrit to sie his leg, quha let you sie it, and ye strakit your hand tenderlie vpoun it; so it fell out, that immediatlie efter, as ye went furth, the great paine slacknit, and ay becam better: Quhilk was done be your witchcraft and devilrie.

X. Item, . . . when Magnus Craigie in Skaebrek was verie seik, Jonet Ingsger, his wyif, going to Hunclet, to seik sum help for him, and by the way shoe met with yow, and told yow of her husbandis seiknes, and ye said vnto hir that ye haid Ursulla Alexanderis snood, quhilk ye haid keipit since ye put hir in hir winding sheit, and said vnto hir that ye wold give it hir, and cause bind it about hir husbandis waist, and if it war the dead manis sting which trublit him, it wold cuir and heale him. Ye said also that Bessie Spence hes ay ane sore head, it is ay pained, and shoe wold faine have this snood fra yow to wear in hir head, for this snood is good for thame that have sore headis: Quhilk sho ressauit from yow, and band it about hir husbandis waist.

XI. Item, . . . That . . . Katherin Barnie, vpoun ane certain day quhen ye wer out of the hous, did goe to your heavie, qnhair it did hing vpon the wall, to sik for ane spindle, and thai-rin fand, bound in a knott within a clout, thrie grassis, whilk shoe reveilit to Annabell Murray, sumtyme spous to Magnus Corse, qua reveilit againe to hir mother Margaret Craigie, and shoe told Hairie Ingsger hir husband thairof, quha took with him Thomas Craigie in Savaskail (being both elderis), they went and found the thrie grassis bound in a knot and lying in your heavie, and shortefter, the said Annabell Mur-ray contractit ane lingring disease, and nevir recouerit thairof quhill sho died.

XII. Item, . . . quhen Katherin Ethay, spous to John Work in Egilschae, was contractit in marriage and proclaimit in the kirk with him, and befoir they wer mairyit together, ye cam to her and said, quhat now ar ye going to dwell in Egilschae, tak my counsale with yow, and ye be wyse, and ye sail not speid the worse; quhen ye ar going out of Rowsay to your awin hous to Egilschae, remember to tak home with yow the wash cog, and the catt of this hous with yow to your awin house.

[This time she was found guilty, and underwent the usual sentence.] *Abbotsford Club Miscellany, vol. i. pp. 171-180.*

[Prefixed to Katherine Craigie's second trial are the following jottings]:

In presens of Mr. George Graham, David Hert, Sim-bister, and the Chamberlane.

Katherine Craigie deponit that Margaret Ranie alias Todlock, heille a kow of John Bellis in Quoysknowis of the baneschaw. And that Cristane Poock, lait servitour to Henrie Ingisgar in Papa, and now with Kowie Insgar, can charme the worme and the fauldseiknes; and that scho vsit the said fauldseiknes to ane ox in Havaskaill, and that scho got for doing thairof a pleat of meill and a blood pudding vpoun the heid of the pleat.

Scho confest the going to the watter, and casting the watter ouer Thomas Irwingis heid.

And that scho learned the charme fra vmquhile Elspeth Linay be the vsing of the stones.

And that scho learned a charme for stemming of blood fra hir vmquhile husband.

                    Abbotsford Club Miscellany, vol. i. p. 171.

Orkney. Trial of Mareoun Cumlaquoy, 1643.—Mareoun "was verie anxious to know when David Cumlaquoy wold sow; and after shoe had herd, shoe went and stood just to his face all the tyme he was sowing: and that yeir his seid failed him, that he culd not sow the thrid of his land, albeit, for quantitie, he had as much as ever." DALYELL, p. 8.

Marion Moir threatened her that she should cause her be

29

burnt if her cow died; but the animal recovered that night: "and her neighbouris ox, struckin with the same diseas as the cow had, presentlie died." —*Ibid.*, p. 109.

She hit a cow thrice "with the skirt of hir coit, and instantly the kow was strukin with a strange seikness." *Ibid.*, p. 390.

She "cam down to Robert Carstair's hous, be sunrysing with milk to his goodmother, shoe nevir vsing to cum thair befoir nor eftir: and as shoe went furth, shoe turnit hirselff thrie severall tymes round witherways, about the fyre: and that year his bear is blew and rottin; and his aittis gives no meall, bot sic as mak all that eit it, hairt seik: albeit, both war fresh and good, quhen he put thame in the yaird." —*Ibid.*, p. 459.

Trial of Elspeth Cursetter, 1629.—Being refused access to the house of a man in Birsay she "sat doun befoir the dure, and said, 'ill might they all thryve, and ill might they speid': and within 14 dayes thairefter, his best horse fell in that same place quhair scho sat, and brack all his bones, and his thie bone gaid throw his bowells to the vther syd of him."
—DALYELL, pp. 33, 34.

She recommended a man to carry the bones of a bird in his clothes to preserve his health: "Get the bones of ane tequhyt, and carry thame in your clothes." —*Ibid.*, p. 150.

Like the fly of Plautus overseeing everything, Elspeth narrating "everie particular disch, and quhat was spoken" at a banquet, declared as her causa scientiae, that she was "on the buird in the liknes of a bie." —*Ibid.*, p. 564.

Trial of Jonet Drever and Katherene Bigland.—Curia Capitalis Vicecomitalus de Orknay et Zetland tenta in Kirkwall per honorabiles viros Henricum Stewart de Carlongyie et Magistrum Wilielmum Levingstoun Vicecomites deputatos dicti Vicecomitatus die vij Junij 1615.

The quhilk day Jonet Drever and Katherene Bigland alias Grewik being pannald indytit and accusit for airt part vseing committing and practizeing of the abhominable and divelishe cryme of witchcraft contened in the particular and severall pointis or dittays gevin in aganes thame Compeirit Robert Coltart procuratour fiscall and desyrit persones to be put to the knawledge of ane assyse.

The said persones being receavit sworne and admittit past al togidder furth of court and ryplie advysit inenterit agane fand and delyverit all in ane voice for the most part the said Jonet Drever be the mouth of Robert Menteth chancelar To be convict and giltie of the fostering of ane bairne in the hill of Westray to the fary folk callit of hir our guid nichbouris And in haveing carnall deall with hir And haveing conversation with the fary xxvj zeiris bygane In respect of her awin confessioun And sicklyk fand and delyverit for the maist part be the mouth of the said chancelar the said Katherene Bigland To be convict and giltie of witchcraft for standing in the style or the kirkzaird of the croce kirk of Westray with drawin knyffis in her hand quhill Marioun Tailzeour hir mother and vtheris that wes in hir companie cam furth of the said kirk the most part of ane nicht Item convictis and fyles the said Katherene for laying of ane duyning and quotidean seiknes upon William Bigland in Swartmiln hir master Item fylit the

said Katherene for practizeing of the said divellische cryme
of witchcraft In going furth under clud of nicht about Can-
delmes last and bringing in to the said William his hous of
wattir as apperit And wesching of the said William his back
therwith And laying him doun saying he wald get guid rest
and lying doun betuix him and the dor having refuissed to ly
in any uther place And the said William haveing walknit with
fear and crying and feilling a thing lyke a ruche scheip abone
him In saying to him be not affrayit for it is the evill spreit
that trublit yow that is going away And in taking of the said
William upone the morne at nicht efter sun setting under the
bankis and wesching of him with salt wattir at that tyme And
fyve or six vthir nichtis therefter quhill he receavit healthe be
hir unlaufull and divelische airt of witchcraft Item fylit the
said Katherene in laying of the seiknes the said William had
upone Robert Broun his servand quha continewit therin almost mad tuo dayis quhill schoe cam and graippit his pulses
and brow and straikit his hair backwards and saying he wald
be weill And casting of the same seiknes immediatlie upon
the said William Bigland And the said Katherene being challengit within the said Ile therfor for taking of the said seiknes
af the said Robert and casiing the same agane upon the said
William In saying if William Bigland livid schoe wald die
And thairfoir God forbid he leive Efter quhais deliverance the
Judges decernis and ordanes the said Jonet Drever to be tane
upone the morne betuix 3 and 4 houris efter nune and scurdg-
it fra the end of the said toun to the uther And thaireftir to be
banisched the cuntre And nevir to returne under the pane of
death And siclyke decernis and ordanes the said Katherene
Bigland to be tane to the heid of the lone the morne at twa
efternune And thair to be bund to a staik and hangit to the

death and burnt to asches And dome gevin heirupone.
                Maitland Club Miscellany, vol. ii., pp. 167, 168.

Shetland. Trial of Jonka Dyneis, 1616.—Being offended with
one named Olave, she "fell out in most vyle cursingis and
blasphemous exclamatiounis, saying, That within few dayis
his bones sould be raiking about the bankis; and sa, within
ane short space thairefter he perished be sey, be hir witchcraft
and devilrie." Next addressing his mother,—"gat Geelis ane
kneel to hir hairt, quhen hir sone Ola dyit! within few dayis
she sail get ane othir: and so within fourtein dayis thairefter
hir vthir sone Mans perished be sey,"   DALYELL, p. 34.

Being questioned after a vision, "could not give answer, bot
stude as if bereft of hir senssis."   —*Ibid.*, p. 443.

The husband of Jonka Dyneis being in a fishing boat at Walls,
six miles from her residence at Aith, and in peril, she was
"fund and sein standing at hir awin hous wall, in ane trans,
that same hour he was in danger; and being trappit, she could
not give answer, bot stude as bereft of hir senssis: and quhen
she was speirit at quhy she wes so movit, she answerit, gif our
boit be not tynt, she is in great hazard—and was tryit so to
be."—*Ibid.*, p. 474.

Geelis, the overseer of Cultmalyndie's wife, failed to obtain
the products of milk, after a quarrel with Jonka Dyneis.
Therefore, "the haill wemen of Hildiswick wer desyrit, as the
forme wes, to kirne, quha come and kirnet, and wes no butter. The said Jonka being desyrit, and having absentit hirself
sundrie tymes, and fleing half a myll frae hir hous; and being
followit and fund be the said Geelis, sche fanyeit hir self seik,

and wes bluiding at mouth and nois—quha broucht hir back agane, and compellit hir to kirne—at quhilk tyme wes gottin sextein merkis butter, quhair befoir wes gottin bot sevin." Also, having got more butter from one cow than a neighbour obtained from fifteen, he "urged hir to kirne with him, efter mony boisting wordis, quha thaireftir gat his butter."—*Ibid.*, pp. 630-31.

Orkney. *Trial of John Faw, gipsy,* 1612.—He gave the gipsies' vocation as "the geveing of thameselfis furth for sorcerie, givearis of weirdis, declareris of fortownis, and that they can help or hinder the proffeit of the milk of bestiall." —*Ibid.*, p. 235.

Westray, Orkney. *Trial of Jonet Forsyth,* 1629.—Intrat upoun pannell Jonet Forsyth, vagabound, dochter to umquhile William Forsyth in Howrnes within the Isle of Westray for the Witchcraftis underwritten.

In the first ye the said Jonet ar indytit and accusit for airt and pairt of the abominable superstitioun and superstitious abusing and disceveing of the people within the said Isle and for practeising of the wicked and devilish pointis of witchcraft and devilrie done by yow. In maner at the tyme and in the places efterspecefeit. And in giving yourselff furth to have sutch craft and knawledge thairof. Thairthrow abusing the people, viz. for slaeing of four gryss's to Manss Peitersone sumtyme in Kirbuster being dweling at the said Manss house for the tyme be your witchcraft and devilrie Quhairby Mareoun Flet be eatting of the said gryss's swallit and becam decraipit in bear seid tyme four or fyve yeiris sene and being confronted with the said Mareoun ye could not denny.

Item ye ar indyttit and accusit for devilish and abominable bewitching of Robert Reid in Coat in Gaird in casting seiknes upoun him, he being upoun the sea, in sick sort That the men that wer in the boit with him were forcit to bring him on shore for fear of death And ye being on the shore at his arryvall He challengit yow for his seiknes and threitened yow In thir words: giff he gott not his health againe It sould be wors nor enough with yow Quhairupoun ye washit him with salt watter Quhairby he recoverit and cam to the sea In health upoun the morne.

Item ye ar Indyttit and accusit for the devilish and abominable bewitching of Thomas Port in Gaird In casting seikness upoun him in februar sex yeiris sene or thairby And being challengit ye cam to visit him and curit him being deadlie diseasit and got maill and cornes for youre paines, and cust his seiknes upoun Michaell Reid in Hewsea his meir quhilk deit as the said Thomas grew quholl, And ye being accusit thairupoun be the said Michaell in vore tyme his wyff and ye being chyding togidder ye could not denny and the meir being oppinit thair was nothing in place of his heart bot ane blob of watter.

Item ye are indyttit and accusit for going to the sea about midsomer sex yeirs sene or thairby at full sea quhen the starrs wer in the firmanent and took ane canfull of salt watter and thairby and be your devilisch practeis ye took away the profeit of Johne Herkas ky.

Item ye are Indyttit and accusit for coming to James Rendallis house in Midbie at Festrensevin four yeairis sene or thairby and having sought ane piece of flesh, and getting bot ane littil piece ye were evill contentit and said that ye sould get mair flesh or ye cam againe, quhilk being hard be the said James wyff, quha reprovit yow notwithstanding be your withcraft and devilrie, vpoun the morne bewitchit tua of his ky quhilk took seiknes and deit within aucht dayes and other thrie within ane quarter of ane yeir.

Item ye are Indyttit and accusit for that the same yeir The said James Rendalls wyff, haiving wantit the proffeit of hir butter, ye cam to the hous, and being challengit be hir for it being sitting be the fyre-syd ane beey cam fleing about youre head quhilk ye tuk and desyrit the guidwyff to put under hir kirin and she sould get her proffeit againe, and becaus the said James took the beey and cust it in the fyre ye was angrie and said although he wald not giff you credit otheris wyld giff you credit.

Item, ye are Indyttit an accusit for that ye cuming to the said James' barne about Candlemes thrie yeirsis sene or thairby, desyrit ane lock corne fra Edward Rendall his sone, quha said thair was nane threachin and ye said ye may give me ane lock, and he pleasit out of the cassie under the unthreachin corne, quhilk wes not sene, and becaus he refusitt to geve yow went to the barne yaird and faddomit ane of the best stacks in the yaird about contrair to the sunns cours quhilk the said Edward seing tald his father, and when the said stack was castin the hail cornes laickit the substance and never did him guid be yor sorcerie and witchcraft.

Item, ye ar Indyttit and accusit That thrie yeiris since or thairby ye cuming to William Setter his hous in Halbreck at

Festrensevin, and seeking ane piece flesh his wyff refusit yow quhairwith ye was angrie and depairting, be your witchcraft and devilrie he losit ane great number of his sheip, sume by running on the sea and otheris deing upoun shore.

Item, ye ar Indyttit and accusit for cuming to Gilbert Hercas als Westray in Poldrit his hous at the time forsaid and seiking ane piece flesh, said to his wyff giff sho wald giff yow ane piece flesh ye wald giff her ane guid sheip luck as ye haid given to sundreis in the Ile quhom ye had maid up. And sho refusand to geve yow any flesh and saying sho wad tak hir to God's luck ye depairted angrie and the said Gilbertis wyff haveing told it to John Walteris wyff ye returnit and reprovit the said Gilbertis wyff and said that sho sould repent that sho told it, quhairupon he losit Twelff horss and meiris within ane halff yeir efter be your witchcraft and sorcerie.

Item, ye ar Indyttit and accusit for that Marjorie Reid, spous to James Drever in Swartmylne being seik and ye cuming to the hous and she challenging yow for hir seiknes and gevin yow ane look corne ye took the seiknes of hir quhairby she was quholl upoun the morne be yor witchcraft and devilrie.

Item, ye ar Indyttit and accusit thrie or four yeiris since ye cuming to Jonet Sinclairis hous in Clet and seiking amas the said Jonet said sho got litill guid by gevin amas to sick folk as sho and that sho wantit the proffeit of ane meill of malt that she was brewing befoir Yule quha ansrit hir that ye knew quha did it and that sho was ower reddie to geve ane drink of her wort and the said Jonet and her servands haveing forgot that any haid gottin any wort ye said ye knew quha had gottin ane drink of it and called her to memorie that Christane Reid in Clett cam in ane maid errand, seiking woft to ane wob and got ane drink and so took the proffeit off the wort with her and she speiring at yow how ye knew that ye said ye knew it well enough and being speirit quhair ye was then and how ye knew it ye said that ye was lying in your bed above Towquoy and knew it weill enough and being speirit quhair ye gat that knawledge ye confest ye gave ane woman callit Monipenney Three quarteris of lyning for learneing of yow.

Item, ye ar Indytait and accusit for that sex yeiris sene or thairby in vore ye faddomit ane stack of bear of sevin faddome perteining to Michaell Reid and that ye took away the substance of the comes thairof and gave it to Robert Reid in Coat of Gaird and being challengit be the said Michaell for it ye took twa meillis of it back againe from the said Robert and gave it him and being challengit be the said Robert Reid, ye took the proffeit of the rest of the stak fra the said Michaell quhairin thair was sevin thrave and ane halff quhairoff he got nothing bot shellings and gave it to the said Robert.

Item, ye are Indyttit and accusit for cuming to the said Michaell Reids hous and the said Michaells wyff said to yow quhat Lucifer learned yow that witchcraft ye ansrit her haid sho not bene euill to yow and haid lettin yow abid with your brother it haid bene telling hir xl. £ and the said Michaells wyff said wer not [for] hir guidmanis maister Michaell Balfour he haid bene deid, ye ansrit he sould not sitt upoun your assyss this yeir and upoun the morne thairefter the said Michaell Balfour fell and braik his coller-bone.

Curia vicecomitatus et Justiciarie de Orknay et Zetland tenta apud Birssay in aula ibid per honorabilem virum Magistrum

Joannem Dick viceconitem et Justiciarium deputatum dict.
vicecomitatus decimo die mensis novembris 1629.
Curia legitime affirmata.

Compeirit Robert Scollay, procuratour ffishall, and produ-cit the dittayes desirit them to be red and the pannell accusit thairupon.

The pannell present dennyit the first point anent the slaeing of the gryss's.

Dennyit the second point anent Robert Reid.

Dennyit the third point anent Robert Port.

Dennyit the fourt point anent the takin of the proffeit of Jon Hercus ky.

Dennyit the haill remanent pointis baith speciall and gener-ali.

The procuratour fishall desyrit the pannell to be put to the knawledge of ane Assyss. The pannell present alleging noth-ing in the contrair was content to undergo the tryell thairof.

Assyss.
[Eighteen names given.]

The witnesses wer admittit and maid faith quhairupon the procuratour fishall askit actis.

Walter Peitersone in Gara bewest depones that Mareoune Flet tald him that she slew the gryss's bot will not say of his conscience that she was the doer of it, and deponed anent Robert Reid that he knew nothing bot as he said to him and the rest that was in the boit.

Michaell Reid in Dyksyd deponed anent Robert Reid con-formis precidenti.

The said Michaell deponed affirmative anent the takin of the seiknes of Thomas Port and casting the same on his meir and that she was the dead of the meir.

John Hercus in Kirbuster deponed that efter the pannell took the salt watter and gave it to Geills Irving he wantit the proffeit of his ky by it and storit never ane calff of fyftene ky be the space of thrie yeirs.

The said Michaell Reid deponed that he saw hir tak the salt watter and four with him and that sho gaid to Geills Irvingis hous with it bot quhat sho wrought by it he knaws not—[also affirms about the fathoming the "beir stak," the conversation of Jonet with his wife, and the breaking of Michael Balfour's collar-bone.]

James Rendall in Midbie deponed that he knew that she spak the words and be her words he kept the skaith of the death of his beastis and deponed affirmative anent the beey conforme to the dittay. And deponed that she was the instrument of the want of the substance of his cornes. Margaret Marwick, spous to Hercules Grot in Clet, deponed that sho was with the guid wyff of Clet and demandit with hir of the said Jonet Forsyth and that she ansrit conforme to the dittay.

[Found guilty and ordained "to be taine be the lockman and conveyit to the place of execution with her hands bund behind her back and worried at ane staik to the dead and brunt in assis."]
From copy of the M.S. of trial by the late George Petrie, Kirkwall.

Orkney. *Trial of Christian Gow,* 1624.—The minister of Westray's servant applied to Christian Gow to cure his master's horse, who "vsit this charme."

> "Three thinges hath the forspokin,
> Heart, tung, and eye, almost;
> Thrie thinges sail the mend agane,
> Father, Sone, and Holie Ghost."
>
> DALYELL, p. 27.

"William Mylne being deidlie seik, and the winding scheit laid at his heid to be put on him," Christian Gow, "by ganting and whispering over the said diseased persone, maid him that he instantlie became wholl and weill." *Ibid.,* p. 124.

Trial of Katherine Grant, 1623.—She went to Henry Janies house "with a stoup in hir hand, with the boddome formest, and sat down ryght foment the said Henrie, and gantit thryce on him:—and going furth he followit hir; and being on the brigstane, scho lukit ouer her shoulder, and turned up the quhyt of her eye, quhair by her divilrie, their fell ane great wecht upoun him, that he was forcit to set his back to the wall; and when he came in, he thoucht the hous ran about with him; and theirefter lay seik ane lang time." *Ibid.,* pp. 7, 8.

She directed Christian, the wife of Thomas Smith, she "being deidlie seik," to fill a vessel with sea-water between sunset and dayset, and putting three stones in it, carefully to preserve silence. But, meeting her husband he commanded her to speak, when he was seized immediately with her distemper, and in peril of his life. *Ibid.,* p. 90.

Being suspected of infecting a child with a disease she was summoned to the house, and on arrival she desired "a cap of water, with ane knyf, and when scho gat it, she movit the knyf in the water, and spat in the cap, and gantit over it, and said,

> The dead upraise,
> To the credell scho gat
> To mend the bairne That bitten was,
> In name of the Father, the Sone,
> and the Haillie Ghaist,
> and commandit the water to be cassin out."

The child recovered.   *—Ibid.*, p. 124.

The mother of a sick child was directed to weigh the child, and taking its weight in barley, to prepare meat for it three successive mornings: then to take the first sup of the meat "and give it to Katherine Sinclairis bairne that was in the hous; quhairvpoun that bairne mendit, and the other bairne grew seik; and quhen the said Katherine heard it, scho was angrie" and threatened the prescriber, "quha bad her set the credell on the other syd of the hous, quher the calff stuid, quhilk the said Katherine did—and sua on the nixt night, the bairne was weill and the calff deit."   *—Ibid.*, p. 107.

To cure James Smithe's horse, she demanded "ane pletfull of corne, with an knyff; efter the recept quhairof scho gaid furth of the house, and efter hir divelish consultation reentering, scho bad the said James big on ane fire in his killogie, and schut his horse bak and foir, to the fyre thryse, and tak ane hedder busome and kendle the same, and sweip the hors thairwith, and syne put him out, and he sould be weill."—*Ibid.*, pp. 126, 127.

Visiting a sick man, she laid her hand "thryse on the point quhair his pane was, and thryse to the eard": and giving him a "cogfull of slaik" to be eat raw on a cake, he recovered daily.—*Ibid.*, p. 388.

She was also charged with approaching a house, "knocking thrie severall tymes at the door, and ane houre betuix everie tyme—and scho not getting in, went away murmuring. Thrie days efter the guid-wyff becam mad." *Ibid.*, p. 390.

She directed that a distempered cow was to be taken backwards into the sea, until washed by nine surges: three handfulls of each were to be laved over her back; when she should be brushed with a bunch of burnt malt straw. *Ibid.*, p. 393.

Trial of Magnus Greive, 1640.—He was reprehended for "going backward in a harrow to see quhat wyff he suld have, and how many childrien." —*Ibid.*, p. 455.

Trial of William Guide, 1616.—William Guide was charged with practiseing, &c., in that Robert Mowat, youngar, haveing fyit his dochter, Jonet Guide, and he detening the said Jonet fra the said Robertis service, obtenit ane decreit before the bailie for hir fie, and cuming to poynd thairfor, the said William promeisit that he sould deir buy that fie, and sa it fell out that his cornes being als guid as ony of his nychtbouris, he could not get na malt of his beir, for the quhilk the said

William, being bayth suspectit and sclanderit, com to the said Robertis barne and tuitcheit baith the cornes freschen and vnfreschen, and baid him mak malt of it, for he said he sould answer that it sould be guid enouch malt, and sa it fell out. . . . For that Sara Stewart, spous to Patrik Boag, haveing caft certane beir quhilk wes givin to him to mak malt of, the beir being sufficient, the malt being returnit fra him, and browen be thame, the aill thairof did stink sa that nane could drink thairof. Thairefter she coft fra Jone Sclatter, in Birsay, ane meill malt, the said William being present, and held vp the malt quhill it wes weyit, and tryit to be sufficient malt. The said Sara reproveing him then for hir first malt went hame to brew the said meill malt quhilk taistit of nathing bot of verie watter, efter the brewing the said Sara and hir husband baith reproveing him for the same, assuiring him that they wald delate him for witchcraft. Immediatelie thairefter he cam to the hous, and that aill that tastit of nathing bot watter of befoir wes sufficient guid aill, and gif thair haid bein ten barrellis thairof it haid bein sauld, or be zeid out of the hous. Item, that haveing aft and dyvers tymes desyreit the len of ane scheret sheilling fra James Hunton in, quha haveing denyit the same hes continuallie sen syne dwynit in seiknes laid on him be his divelrie and witchcraft. Item, for this yeir on Beltane day last in the morneing, he cuming to William Kirknes' hous, and desyreing ane cashie of hay fra him, quhilk being given to him, immediatlie thairefter that same day ane foill of the said William Kirknessis died, and on the morne ane meir with foill lykwayes dyit, and his haill guidis hes continuallie decayit sen syne be his divelrie and witchcraft. Item, that he and his dochter haveing ane lamb going in Mans Futtspurres corne, and about his hous, cuming in to the said Mans, his stable, his hors strampit vpon the leg of the said lamb and brak it, for the quhilk the said William prayit evill for the said Mans, and that same yeir his four hors and his oxen died, quhilk wes done be his divelrie and witchcraft.

ROGERS, v. iii. pp. 299-300.

Helen Hunter, Inswoman in Brugh, 1643.—[To ascertain whether the properties of milk were abstracted by one deceased or surviving, she directed the owner to milk the cow over an inverted cup, in the pail, when the rise of a bubble on removing the cup indicated a delinquent deceased.]—DALYELL, p. 514.

[Spinning a black rock is alluded to as pernicious to cattle, but no particulars given.]   —*Ibid.,* p. 256.

Trial of Jonet Irving, 1616.—The devil while in the form of a woman, on hearing Christ's name uttered ran "out at the holl of the door lyk a black catt."   —*Ibid.,* p. 554.

Trial of Helene Isbuster, 1635.—It was charged against her "that in Paba, the glaid having slaine some fowles, ye commandit him to sit downe on the rigging of the house, quha sat till he died." The charge does not seem to have been proved; but the culprit was convicted of charming mice into a stack, where all were found dead: and she confessed having pronounced some words to expel them from their previous haunt.—Ibid., p. 270.

A man was utterly ruined by nine knots cast on a blue thread, and given to his sister.—Ibid., p. 307.

Shetland. Trial of Katherine Jonesdochter, 1616.—It was alleged against her that she "wisheit in her mind" that her husband's infirmities might be transferred to a stranger.

Ibid., p. 6.

She was also accused of being able to transfer disease merely by wishes and grasping the hand of the intended sufferer.—

Ibid., p. 106.

She saw the "Trowis ryse out of the kirkyeard of Hildiswick, and Holiecross Kirk of Eschenes, and on the hill called Greinfaill." They came to any house where there was "feasting, or great mirrines and speciallie at Yule." —*Ibid.*, p. 532-33.

[Cf. II. a, "YULE."]

Orkney. Trial of James Knarstoun, 1633.—He came to cure a woman in Dairsay of the "bainschaw" bringing "ane litle pig of oyle, maid of Mekillwort, as he himself allegit." He took such water as was in the house, "and washit hir feit fra hir kneis doun, and hir airmes, nobody being besyd bot ane litle sone of his awin. The watter being in ane daffok, shoe perceavit that their was twa or thrie stones in the watter, quhilk he took and pat about hir kneis, and vsit some few word is. Efter as he haid washit her feit and airmes, he dryit them, and rubbed of the oyle againe quhilk he had brocht with him, beffor the fyre: and becaus the oyle was not stark enuch, he gat some aquavite to mak it starker the next time." Repetition of this remedy within fifteen days cured the patient.*Ibid.*, p. 153. He took "ane stone for the Ebb, another for the Hill, and the thrid for the Kirk-yaird: and thairefter be seithing of thame fyre hott in water, and laying of thame above the lintell of the doore for the space of ane nicht and more: and then taking and puting of thame in ane tub full of cold water, vsing some wordis knowen vnto himselff—thairby to understand be quhat stone that suld mak the bullering and noise, as is maist fairfull to be sein, [be] quhat spirit it is that the person diseasit hes the disease: and so to call thame home againe."—*Ibid.*, pp. 508-9.

For "cuiring of dyvers and sundrie persounes," water was taken at midnight from St. Mary's well at Kirkbuster, and the patient washed between dawn and sunrise, wherein the diviner, probably cast melted lead, "throw the bowle of ane pair of cheiris thrie sundrie tymes, at ilk time saying thir wordis, 'in the name of the Father, Sone, and Holie Ghost.' "—*Ibid.*, p. 511.

The issue of distempers was divined from liquified substances, such as lead or wax congealed in water. Patrick Hobie's daughter being sick, he had promised "to cast her heart-caik of lead quhen shoe suld come to him."   *Ibid.*, p. 511.

While leading peats darkness overspread the sun "and thairwith a monstrous cloak cam fleing and buzing about, and entrit in at his mouth, and he fell to the ground on his face and grew blew—it was als great as ane of the little birds that fieis in the yeird."   —*Ibid.*, p. 565.

Trial of Cirstane Leisk, 1643.—After offending and wrangling with Cirstane Leisk, a man immediately "fell deidlie sick that he could not stir him." When brought by menaces "to the hous quhair he lay, and shoe looking on the said Alexander, he presentlie start to his feit, and went to the foot-ball."—*Ibid.*, p. 59.

A man sickened while she spread her hand over his back. When this was repeated, the pain ceased "and immediately he became whole."   —*Ibid.*, p. 61.

Trial of Oliver Leask, 1616.—On a cow giving a deficiency of milk, grass from the spot whereon the pail stood, was to be thrown among the milk to avert recurrence of the like.

Ibid., p. 126.

Trial of Magnus Linay and Geillis Sclaitter his wife, 1616.—Magnus Linay charged with, &c., inasmuch that his sone being keiping his ky, and suffering thame to go in Robert Grayis corne in Watle, the said Robert finding his ky in his corne, gave his sone ane cuff, quhilk the said Magnus perceaving fleitt with the said Robert thairfoir, and assuirit him that he sould repent that straik, and that same day being about lambmes tua yeiris syne or thairby, the best hors that he had dyit, and his haill bestiall, hors, nalt, and sheip hes dyit, and nathing thryves with him sen syne.—ROGERS, vol. iii. p. 300.

They were accused of having accompanied the Egyptians [Gypsies], and of having "lernit to take the proffeit ot thair nyghtbouris cornis and ky of the saids Egyptians, as the captane of thame declarit."   —DALYELL, p. 236.
Trial of Cirstain Marwick, 1643.—While a woman was milking her cow Cirstain "lookit in ower the duir, quhairvpoun the calf died presentlie, and the kow fell seik, that schoe wold

nether eat nor yield milk." —*Ibid.*, p. 5.

While Margaret Craigie was recovering, Cirstain Marwick "straikit hir hand ower the said Margaret's breast and that same night" she died. —*Ibid.*, p. 52.

Trial of Katherin Miller, 29 May, 1633.—A woman labouring under an extraordinary disease, compelling her to "creip on hands and feit," recovered presently and received as good health as ever, from the hand of Katherin Miller laid on her head. —*Ibid.*, p. 61.

Shetland. Trial of Marion Peebles, alias Pardone, Spous to Swene in Hildiswick.—In the first, you the said Marion Peebles alias Pardone, is indytit and accusit for the sinful and damnable renouncing of God, your Faith and Baptism, giving and casting of yourself, body and soul in the hands of the Devil, following, exercising, using and practising of the fearfull and damnable craft of Witchcraft, Sorcerie, and Charming, in manner, following, viz.

In the first, you are Indytit and accusit for coming in the month of Imvjc [1600] and thirty years, to the house of John Banks in Turvisetter, and Janet Robertson his spouse, with a wicked, devilish and malicious intention to cast Witchcraft and Sickness upon them; and missing the said Janet there, for going to Sursetter, where she then was, and after cursing and scolding her, telling her that she should repent what she had done to your daughter and good-son. And for that immediately with the word, ye, by your devilish art of witchcraft, did cast sickness upon the said Janet, who, immediately upon your departure, fell in an extraordinary and unkindly sickness, and lay eight weeks, taking her shours and pains by fits, at midday and midnight, and so continued most terribly tormented; her said sickness being castin upon her by your said devilish witchcraft, during the said space, until the said John Banks came to you and threatened you, at which time ye gaif him a gullion of silver, to hold his peace and conceal the same, promising to him that nothing should ail his wife. And thereafter, for that ye sent her ane cheese of the breadth of ane loof, composed by your said devilish art of witchcraft, with ane junke-roll, and desiring her the said Janet to eat the same, when (whereof the said Janet refused to eat), yet immediately she grew well, but two of her kine died, the said sickness being castin upon them by your said wicked and devilish art of Witchcraft.

2. Likeas also, you are indytit and accusit, for that by your said art of devilish witchcraft, ye did, upon the recovery of the said Janet, cast the same sickness upon Marion Banks, sister to the said John Banks, which troubled her after the same manner, tormenting her for twenty days, until that one Osla in Olsnafirth, coming to you, by direction of the said John Banks, and warned you hereof, whereupon by your said devilish witchcraft, the said sickness was taken off the said Marion and casten upon a young cow of the said John's, which took wodrome, and died within twenty-four hours.

3. Ye the said Marion are indyted for that you being very shroudly suspected, and commonly bruited as a common witch, ye coming along upon some of your said devilish and wicked intentions to umquil Edward Halcro in Overure,

quhair he was dichting bear to steep for malt, you being of wicked intention, by your said devilish craft, did unto the said making of malt, and he suspecting you, after he had reproved you for minding you about him, you said to him all would be well touching the said making, as it fell out: so taking upon you and acknowledging by your wordis your power in the said wicked and devilish art of witchcraft. That, after that, he being there scrowing come, and ye persisting in your said wicked and devilish intentions to undo and provock the said Edwd. you did thereby marr and undo twa whole makings of the said bear, quhilk never did good.

4. The said Marion is indytit and accusit for that in April 1641, the said Edward coming to your houss, after ye had urged him to take meat, he took resolution to go to the war having not intention before, and going with Sueno your husband to the gio heid where they were usit to go down, he being affrayit to go down first, desyrit your husband to go befoir him, quha refusing to go, the said Edward went, whereon he going down and stepping upon a stone which was ever a sure step befoir, ye the said Maron maid the said stone to lows and fail down with him, whereby his life was in great perill, yet saved to the admiration of all the beholders. And ye being accusit for taking the said occasion and cryme upon you, anserit that it was not for his gud, but for Helen Thomson his spous gud that he was savit.

5. Ye the said Marion are indyttit and accusit for that ye did cast ane terrible and fearful madnes and sicknes upon ane Madda Scuddas-doughter, your awin friend, becaus she wold not byd with you, quhairon she continuit most terriblie tor-

mentit, and throw the torment of the said disease, she was causit many times to run upon her awin sister that keepit her, and divers, so as to have devorit them in her madnes, and so continuit a zeir and half ane zeir, till she, being counsallit, ran upon the said Marion and drew blood of you, within James Halcros Hows, biting twa of your fingers till they bled, whereupon the said Madda Scudda-doughter recoverit of her disease, and came to her ryt sinces.

6. Ye the said Marion Pardoun ar indyttit and accusit for that James Halcro in Hildiswick having a cow that ye alledged had pushed a cow of yours, ye in revenge thereof, maid the said James his cow milk nothing but blood, whereas your awin cow had no harm in her milk; whereupon they suspecting you, shewit the said bloody milk to Marion Kilti your servant, quha desyrit of you the same bloody milk for Goddis caus to shew you, and said she houpit the cow sould be weil; quhilk having gotten, and coming therewith to your hous, and shawing it to you, thereafter the cow grew weil, thairby shewing and proving your said devilish practyce of the art of witchcraft.

7. Ye the said Marion are indytit and accusit for that you having anno 1642 zeirs hyrit ane cow from Androw Smith, younger in Hildiswick, which ye keepit fra the bull, when she wald have taken bull, and the said Andro getting knowledge thereof, causit the same to be brought to the bull and bullit against your will. The next year when she calved, ye took away her proffeit and milk, so that she milked nothing but water, quhilk stinked and tasted of sharn a long time, till that you comming by the said Andro his hous, he suspecting you,

caused you to milk her and look to her, after which doing, immediatlie the said cows milk cam to its own nature.

8. Ye the said Marion ar indyttit and accusit for that ye coming by ane pies of grass quhairin Andro Smith elder in Videfield had six kine tederit, quhairintil ye went, and out of whilk grass, ye and your son, after ye had lousit and taken the kyne, fell in sculding with and abusit the said Andro, and said to him that he sould not have so many kine to eat grass and milk the next zeir; according to the quhilk wordis, sa it fell out thereafter; for that by your said wicked and devilish art of witchcraft, the said hail kyne died befoir the next half yeir, all fat and gudlike by that same order, as they were lousit by you on tedder, beginning at the first cow, (quhilk was ane black cow, qlk ye lousit, qlk died 20 days before Yule, fat and tydie,) and so furth in succession the rest, by your sd devilish witchcraft.

9. Ye coming to the said Andro Smyth elder, and desyring him len you ane of his hors, to go to Urafirth to lead peatis, qlk he refusit to do, ye out of a wicked and malicious heart said to him that he would repent it; quhereupon ye by your sd wicked and devilish airt of witchcraft, and for outting of your malice, and for keeping of your said devilish promeis, within aught days thereafter did kill ane of his best worke hors, and within half ane zeir thereafter other three of his sd hors; thairby shewing baith in your words and deeds, your wicked and devilish skill concerning the practise of the fursd devilish and abhominable airt of witchcraft.

10. Ye being suspectit to have castin sickness upon the said Andro Smith elder his oy, qrof she lay long benumed and senseless, ye coming tyme foirsd to the hous of Overure, and

they challenging and quarrelling you therefor, ye fell into cursing and swearing and went to the dore, qr ane calf was standing in the dore besyd you, qrupon in your sd wicked and devilish malice, be your sd detestable craft of witchcraft, ye did cast sickness that it presentlie run mad, cracy, and died.

11. Ye the said Marion are indyttit and accusit for coming to Andro Erasmusson's house in Eshaness, qr he having ane cow three days calved befoir, qrupon as ye luikit, ye immediately be airt and devilrie cast sickness that she immediatlie crap togidder, that no lyf was looked for her; till they sent for you, and causit you lay your hand upon her, qrupon scho then immediatlie recoverit, and was weil.

12. Likeas [ye the sd Marion] to cullour and extenuat your sd craft, alledging that ye wantit the profit of your kyne, qlk was not true, but onlie to tak occasion, by your sd wicked and devilish airt of the profit of the said Andro his kyne, came to his hous in July therefter, and efter cursing his wyf, quha shawed you the milk of her kyne, desirit her to caus Usla Sinclar, her servant woman, to go with you to the kerne, qlk she did. Qrby ye touk away with you the profeit of the sd Andro his kyne until the space of throttein dayes; till the sd Andro his wyf went to your hous, and shewit you the milk and butter, and maid publication yrof to the nybours, and immediatlie thereafter gat back her profeit of baith her milk and butter.

[13.] Ye ar indytit and accusit for that ye cam to Thomas in Urabister, and desyrit a quoyach cow of his of four yeir old to hyre, qlk was with calf then, whereof he maid you half a grant, but not the full, until he could advise with his Mrs, the gud wyf of Urafirth, quha would not consent, and becaus ye gat her not, ye outscoldit him and wer verie angrie. And in revenge of his sd refusal, immediatlie yrafter ye cas seeknes upon the sd cow, qlk being at the hill with utheris of his kyne, scho tuik a wodroam or madnes and cam scouring hame frae the rest to the byre dere, brak up the saim and went in, having her head thrawin backward to her back, that four people could not get it back, and thereby dyed throw the sd diseas, cassin on her by your sd airt, working and witchcraft.

14. Lykeas ye not being in your devilish and wicked mynd enough revenget and satisfyct ye be the same your craft, devilrie, and witchcraft, within six weeks yrefter, cast the lyke seiknes upon ane uther cow of the sd Thomas his kyne, whereby scho also died mad and in wodram.

15. Ye the sd Marion are indyttit and accusit for that in anno 1634, at Michelmes, when the cornes were taking in, the sd Thomas in Urabister having aught piere of hors and mairs gaing on the riggs of Olnais firth, ye cam furth with a staff to ding away his hors, qn ye fell and hurt your knee, whereupon ye, to revenge yourself, and to assyth your wicked and malicious heart and mynd, did, by your foirsd airt of witchcraft and devilrie, caus that within aught dayis thereafter his best hors died, and thereafter before Candlemes uther sex hors and mares.

At Scalloway, the 15th March, 1645 zeirs.

We the Moderator and remanent Brethren of the Presby-terie

of Zetland, being conveened day and place forsaid and having examined the above wreattin process, doe find and declare the poyntis . . . lawfullie prowin to be witchcraft, and yrfor the pairtie guiltie worthy of death be the law of God and the law of the kingdome, and requyris you judges to put them to the knawledge of ane assyse, and minister justice upon them accordinglie, as ye will be ansrable to God, his Maijestie and Counsel, and to discharge of your deutie heeranent.

NICOL WHYTE, Moderater.
W. ROBERT MURRAY, Clk.

Fytts. Item, ye the said Marion Peebles alias Pardoun, ar indyttit and accusit for that at Candlemiss or thereby 1643, on ane Sunday, ye coming into the hous of James Halcro in Hildiswick, where Andro Broun then wis for the time, and falling into contest, and fletting with him about linching ane boat, ye, being enraged, set your venefical malice against him, and cursit him with many wicked and execrable words, and by your damnable and venefical heart wishit and cravit ill may so befall him: whereupon by your develish airt and craft of witchcraft ye bewitched him, and cast sickness upon him immediately that he fell in a deadlie sickness and diseas.—That upon Munday next hereafter, he did contract sa vehement and deadlie diseas and sickness, tormentit thereby fra the croun of his head to the sole of his fute, that there was no lyff expectit of him. Quhairfor his nybers, knawing your detestable brute of witchcraft, and your pouir at your said practising, and that on whomsoever your cursed charm fell, sum notable and extraordinar mischieff and evile followit to yame, they did advys him to send for you, to shaw that there wis na lyff for him, and that they all suspectit you for casting the samin upon him. Quhairupon, after many dinyellis to cum and see him, at last you cam to him, quhen shewing you his diseas and sicknes, togidder with the racking pain thereof, imputit by him and utheris to be your act and doing, Andro thaerfor prayit you to lay your hand upon him, which you wold not do, nor be na intreatti nather of him nor of your nybures moved thereto till that they all that wer in the hous, being wearied of your refusal, went furth grivet, and prayit you for Goddis cause to lay your hand upon him; and then at last, being movit thereto, using your said venefical and damnabil charms and witchcraft, ye did uncover his leg, and pat your finger thereon, and on the ground three severall tymes, to and fra; qrby immediatlie, by your said airt of witchcraft and charms, he fell, and said his pein and diseas was desolvit frae the crown of his head to the sole of his fute; at qlk tyme he was before her tutch sa heavyly diseased frae top to toe, through all his body, with swelling in his handes, lykwise armis, leges and knees, that he was unable to move or turn himself in the bed; but after your said tutch, he became able to sit up, and turn himself in the bed, and within twa dayes, was fullie recoverit, and went furth. Quhilk sudden recoverie, togidder with your forme and manner of charming, and cureing of be your said tutch and charmes being spread abrod amang your nybers, and the said cuming to your ears, about 14 days after his recoverie, ye said to your nybbers emgrace on them that had bewitched you, that wald not witch you oer the banks; quhairupon immediatlie again he fell again in the sd sicknes wors than befoir, and paynet away with sic extremetie of sicknes, that he sent you againe, desyring meat out of your hand; and after long intreatie, ye wald not cum to him with it, least your witchcraft and charmes again sould cum to lyt, but

send wt Swene your husband, ane bannock, after long stryv-
ing betwix the sd Swene and you, qlk of you sould give the
samin to him; qlk he having eaten, he again recoverit presentlie thereafter, and the sd sicknes was cassin be you upon ane
cow, pertaining also to Andro, qlk then died.

Item, ye the sd Marion ar indyttit and accusit for that, you
bearing and deadlie and veneficall malice in your heart
agains the sd umquill Edward Halcro in Overure, and in-
crissing your malice and divclish intentiones of your wicked
heart, and taking occasion to renew and bring your wicked
intention by your sd wicked airt of witchcraft, to work his
ruyine and death,—(being set on edge be a speitch spoken
be him to the sd Swene your husband, when he was castin
peates to him in Voir last year, as the sd Andro Brown also
was castin peatis to him, having callit to your sd husband,
and bade him go to you, to desyre you to go to your pobe, the
devill, and bid him loose ane knot, that the sd Andro Brown
myt be able, being then verie waik, to cast out his bank of
peates:)—qrupon ye and the sd Swene being angrie, awaitting
your occasion to practise your said abominable airt and craft
of witchcraft, to distroy and put down the sd Edward Halcro,
and having covenantit and conversit with the devill to bring
the saim to pass, (as ane declaration of umquhill Jvenit Fraser,
witch, whom you desyrit the devill to move her to assist you
doth prove, qlk she both before and after her conviction did
testiffie,) ye be your sd wicked, detestable, abhominable and
develish airt of witchcraft, being transformed in the lyknes
of an pellack quhaill, (at the [counsel of the said Swene,] and
be your consent and wish, the devill changing your spirit, qlk
fled in the same quhaill;) and the said Edward being at sey

with . . . [other three men], all four in ane fishing boat coming fra the sey at the north bankis of Hildiswick, on ane fair
morning, ye did cum under the said boat and overturnit her
with ease, and drowned and devourit thame in ye sey, right
at the shore, when there wis na danger utherwayis, nor hazard to have cassin them away, it being sik fair widder, as said
is. Lykwais when the said umquill Edward wis fund with the
said umquill 1 and you and the said Swino your husband wir
sent for, and brought to see thame, and to lay your hands on
thame dayis after said death and away casting, quhaire their
bluid was evanished and desolved from every natural cours
or caus to shie and run, the said umquill Edward bled at the
collir bain or craig bane and the said in the hand and fingers,
gushing out bluid thereat to the great admiration of the beholders and revelation of the judgment of the Almytie. And
by which lyk occasionis and miraculous works of God, made
manifest in murders, and the murderers, whereby be many
frequent occasiones brought to light, and the murderers be
the sd proof brought to judgment, convicted and condemned,
not onlie in this kingdom, also this countrie, but lykwayis in
maist forrin Christiane kingdomis; and be so manie frequent
precedentis and practising of and tuitching murderis and
murdereris notourlie known, so that the foirsaid murder and
witchcraft of the saidis persons, with the rest of their com-
panions, through your said husbands deed, art, part, rad and
counsall, is manifest and cleir to not onlie through and by
the foirsaid precedents of your malice, wicked and malishis
practises, by witchcraft, confessionis and declaration of the
said umquill Janet Fraser, witch, revealed to her as said is, and
quha wis desyrit by him to concur and assist with you to the
doing thereof; but lykwayis be the declaration and revelation

of the justice and judgmentis of God, through the said issueing of bluid from the bodies, qrby booth you and your said husband ar found takin, and proven in the art of your said witchcraft and murder.

Lykeas ye the said Marion, indyttit and accusit as ane common rank witch, charmer and deceaver, and quaha wer all your dayes, then xl years and more been so report and halden, bearing yourself sa, Consulting, riving with the devill in his caus, who did change lyknis appearing to you severallie; for that ye being cuming fra Brecknon to Hildiswick, in the month of last, quhen you wirr to be apprehendit and sent in for the foirsayid crymes to suffer, the devill there in the way, did converse and appear to you, both in your going to and frae Breckon and Hildiswick, in the lyknes of twa corbies, ane on every side of you, clos at your sides, going and happing alongis the way with you to Hildiswick, and stayid where you went, not leaving you three quarters of a mile, till Mr. Robert Ramsay overtuik you, when they came full flyght to the sey, and the corn land and hills; he then did challenge you anent the saidis corbies, of the cause of thair so far accompanying you, sa neir and sa far away, it not being the natuir of wyld fuillis to follow sa far, and keep pace sa neir approaching ony man or woman. Ye then did cast a glos upon it, saying they smellit bread on you, quhilk made them, (to quhom ye sayd ye was casting bread) to come,—quhilk wis onlie a lie maid by you, conceeling. At your returne they continuit with you, and conversit ut supra, als far back agane as scoir and threttein. As lykways you have not onlie behavid yourself as sayd is, as ane common rank witch, alwayis giving yourself to charmes, and never knowing the trew God, and quhom the truly sentifyed

Chryst ar, not sa much as to learne the Lordis Prayer, nor to repeat the samen in all your lyfe time, but ar reprovit from God; has given yourself, boith saul and bodie, to serving the Devill, and bund up in him, that ye will not muster power, nor will cast off the Devill, sa mutch as to follow learning to repeat the Lordis Prayer amangist Goddis ministers and children, but ar, and has been all your dayis ane wicked, devilish, fearful and abhominable curser; quhaver ye ever cursed, ane [and] them ye disendit and wishit evil to, everie evil, seeknes, herme and death followit thereupon, throw your diabolical tongue, witchcraft and cursing. And hes ever behavit yourself as ane common witch and charmer, taker away of your nyber's profeits of their roumes, landes, cornes, grass, butter, kye, sheip, and wul, and a charmer and healer of sum, and caster of sicknesses upon uthers, and everie way living a damnable, wicked and diabolical lyff, contrarie to God and his commandments.1 Quhilk you cannot deny, and quhair-foir you the said Marion ought and sould undergo the tryal of ane assyse, and being convictit and adjudged thairfoir to the death, and your hail landis, if any be, ye have foirfattit, and your moveabil goods escheat, and inbrought to his Majesty's use, conforme to the lawis and daylie practise of this realme . . .

[21 March, 1644. She was found guilty by the assyse of] the hail poyntis of dittay agains her, boith general and special, except theft of Thomas of Urabister not provin, and anent Ed-

61

ward Halcro's malt, quherein they rest clauseure, and, They all in one voice ffylls her of the haill poyntis of dittay producit, and remittis sentens to the Judges, and dome to the dempster.

The Judges adjudges and decerns the pannell to be taken brought hence to the place of execution to the Hill of Berrie, and there wyryt at ane stak, and brunt in ashes, betwix and 2 aftirnoone, qlk Andro of Offir, dempster, gave for dome.

HIBBERT, pp. 593-602.

Orkney. *Trial of Jonet Reid.*—Intrat vpoun pannell, Jonet Reid, for the abhominable superstitioun of vsing and practeis-ing of the Witchcraftis vndirwrittin, viz.:

Ye, the said Jonet Reid, ar indytit and accusit for airt and pairt of the contraveining of the tennour of the act of Parlia-ment, maid be our vmquhile dread sovirane ladie, Marie, be the grace of God, Queen of Scottis, with the adwyse of the Thrie Estates, in the nynth Parliament: That, quhair they be-ing informit of the heavie and abhominable superstitioun vsit be dyverse of the leidges of this realme, be vseing of witch-craft, sorcerie, and necromancie, and credens gevin therto in tymes bygane againest the law of God; and for awoyding and awayputting of all sik superstitioun in tyme cumming, it was statut and ordanit, be the Queenis maiestie and Thrie Estates forsaidis, That na persoun or personis, off quhatsumeuer es-tat, degrie, or conditioun they be of, tak vpoun hand, in any tyme therefter, to vse any maner of witchcraftis, sorceries, or necromancies, or giue thame selffis furth to haue sik craft or knowledge, thairthrow abuseand the people, vndir the paine of death: And trew it is, and of veritie, that ye, the said Jonet, hes contraveinit the tennour of the said act of Parliament, be vseing and practeising of witchcraftis, sorceries, divina-tiounes, and superstitious charmeingis, and in geving zour selff furth to haue sik craft and knowledge, and in companie keiping with the devill, zour maister, at dyverse and sundry places and tymes, and thairthrow abuseand the people, in maner following: And thairfoir, and for vsing and practeis-ing of the said abhominable superstitioun, aught and suld be adjudgit to the death, in example of vtheris to doe the lyk.

I. And in special, ye ar indytit and accusit for airt and pairt of the abhominable superstitioun, in that about aught or nyne yeiris since, William Kirknes in Pow, being bigging his bear stak, ye cam to him, and offered him ane grass, as ye callit it, but to his appearance, nothing but ane litle quantitie of quhyt moss or fogge, and baid him put it in his stack, affirmeing that it suld mak him keip the profeit of his cornis, so that none suld be abili to tak it from him, which, notwithstanding, he refusit to doe, saying that he saw no profit in it; quhair-vpoun ye went away discontented.

II. Item, ye ar indytit and accusit, That about the tyme for-said, ye being ins-woman in the said William Kirkness hous, as he was ryseing in the morneing, he hard yow say to your doghter, wha was onlie with yow in the fyrehous ye being in the meantyme drying corne with ane hott stone one ane flak-kit, I am drying this corne to [the] devill; and with that word, he stepped out of the celle where he lay, and saw incontinent the stone and the whole corne ye war drying, flie throw the hous, so that thair culd be nevir ane bit of the stane, or ane pickle of the corne, be sein againe. Quhilk was done be your

63

witchcraft and devilrie, and quhilk ye offerit in ane sacrifice to the devill your maister.

III. Item, ye ar indytit and accusit, That about aught zeiris since or thairby, Robert Sinclair of Nether Gersand, being impotent at that tyme, as he gaue it out himselff, ye gaue Margaret Sinclair, naturall dochter to the said Robert, some liquour like water in ane stoup, and directit hir to put it twa or thrie seuerall tymes in his meat, and he having suppit thairof, within ane night, or at most twa, after, he fand himselfe restorit to his wountit vigour and abilitie; and William Kirknes hearing how the said Robert was restorit, jesting with yow, askit yow how ye haid helped Robert Sinclair his father in law? ye answerit, If he haid cum to yow befoir he was married, ye suld haue helpit him than alsweill as ye haue done now; quhilk was be your witchcraft and devilrie.

IV.—Item, ye ar indytit and accusit, That,1 yeiris since or thairby, Robert Sinclair in Gerssand, being efter he haid married his secund wyif, sore trublit in his sleip with apparitiounes of his ffirst wyiff, which wexit him and disquietit him verie much, he was advysit be yow to goe to his first wyfis grave, and to chairge hir to ly still and truble him no moir.

V. Item, ye ar indytit and accusit, That about nine yeiris since or thairby, John Kirknes in Housgar, being heavilie diseasit, ye cam to his hous, and said to his wyif, Your husband hes the beanschaw, and gif ye will I can help him: Quhairvpoun his wyif cam to him, and desyrit him to ryis, and cum to the fyre hous, quhich he did at his wyifis desyr, and ye said to him, Guidman, if ye will, I sall charme yow of the boneshaw: And he consenting, ye gropped all the joyntes of one of his sydes with her [your] hand, and spake certain wordis ower him, and causit Katherin Kirknes, his servant woman for the tyme, repeat everie word efter yow, at your directioun, in presens of his wyif and servant woman.

VI. Item, ye ar indytit and accusit, That, yeiris since or thairby, ye charmed Elspeth Sinclair, spous to William Kirknes, of the boneshaw (as ye callit it); and that ye vsit besyd wordis, nyne blue stones, quhilk shoe did put in ane vessell with water, twitching her joyntis with each of the severall stones, which ye keipit in your lap, and went fourth with; and efter washed her with the water that was in the wessell in which the stones lay.

VII. Item, ye are indytit and accusit, That, yeiris since or thairby, ye charmed Henrie Sowie, servitour to Alexander Linklater in Housgar, of the boneshaw; and that ye causit ane sone of the said Alexander repeat the charme after yow; and that ye vsit water and stones, as is aforesaid, whilk was alreddie confest be yow; and the said Henrie, being vnabill to stirr out of his bed for the space of fourtein dayis befoir, recoverit his health, and was abili for his work within twa dayis efter, as ye haid said the charme ower him; whilk was done by your witchcraft and devilrie.

VIII. Item, ye ar indytit and accusit, That, yeiris since or thairby, that ane of Alexander Linklatteris children in Housgar being leane and ill lyke, ye said that the child haid the hart cake; and that gif ye pleasit ye wold cast the hart cake, and sie what wold become of him; which ye did in this maner: Ze took ane pott with water in it, and laid the tonges athwart the mouth of the pott, and than laid ane codd aboue the tonges, and set the child on it; thairefter ye took ane seif and set [it] on the childis head, and set ane cogge full of water in the seive, and then laid ane woll scheir on the coggis mouth, and then ye took lead and put it in ane iroun lamp, and meltit it, and powrit it throw the boul of the scheir into the water thrie severall tymes devining throw the lead whither the child wold recover or not; and quhen ye haid done all, ye gaue the child ane drink of the said water, and said he wold be weill; [but as yit the child is not].

IX. Item, ye are indyted and accusitt That, yeiris since or thairby, ye vsit the haill particular charme aboue-written, in all poyntis, with ane child of Robert Sinclairis in Nether Gersand.

X. And generallie, ye are indytit and accusit for airt and pairt of the vsing and practeising of witchcraftis, sorceries, divinatiounes and charmes, as particularlie abouewritten; and in geving your selff furth to haue sik craft and knowledge, thairthrow abuseand the people; and that by your cursingis and imprecatiounes, ye wronge both man and beast. Quhilk evillis ar brocht to pas be the power and working of the devill your maister: And thairfoir ye aught and suld vndirly the law, and be adjudgit to the death thairfoir, in example of vtheris to doe the lyk.

Abbotsford Club Miscellany, vol. I., pp. 181-185.

Trial of Jonet Rendall, 1629.—In the ffirst ye the said Jonet ar

Indyttit and accusit for airt and pairt of the abominable sup-
perstitioun and suppperstitious abusing and deceiveing of the
people and for practeising of the wicked and devilish pointis of witchcraft and sorcerie done by yow in maner at the
tymes and in the places efter specifiet and in geving yourselff
furth to have sick craft and knowledge thairthrow abuseing
the people, To Wit, Twentie yeiris since and mair ye being
above the hill of Rendall having soucht charitie and could not
have it the devill appeirit to you, Quhom ye called Walliman,
claid in quhyt cloathis with ane quhyt head and ane gray
beard, And said to you He sould learne yow to win almiss be
healling of folk and quhasoever sould geve yow almiss sould
be the better ather be land or sea. And these yt gave yow not
almiss sould not be healled and ye haveing trustit in him and
entering in pactioun with him, He promeisit to yow that quhasoever sould refus yow almiss and quhatever ye craved to
befall thame sould befall thame, and thairefter went away in
the air from you, Quhairby ye practeised many and sindrie
pointis of witchcraft and devilrie and speciallie the pointis
following.

Item ye are Indyttit and accusit for cuming fyve yeiris since or
yrby to Manss Work in Windbrek his Wyff and haveing askit
almiss of hir and sho refusand ye said sho sould repent it, and
within aught dayes cfter ane of his ky fell over the craig and
deit be your witchcraft and devilrie conforme to the pactioun
maid betwix yow and your walliman, and within thrie dayes
ye being reprovit be the said Manss wyff ye said that if sho
sould geve yow the wyt of it wors sould cum of it and that
she sould ather run upoun the Sea or then ane war cast sould
befall hir. Quha being quholl then deit within thrie dayes be

your witchcraft and devilrie.

Item ye ar Indyttit and accusit for cuming at Candlmes last to Edward Gray in Howakow hous and shakin your blanket as it wer aganes the hous and Patrick Gray his sone having cum furth and seing yow cald his father and fearing your evill went to the barne and geve yow ane look corne and on monday nicht thairefter Tua meiris deit both at once in the stable and that the said Patrick took seiknes the same hour he saw yow and dwyned thrie quarteris of ane yeir and deit, and ye being send foir befoir his death to see him, He being dead befoir and haveing laid his death on you, how shone ye cam in the cors having lyin ane guid space and not having bled any, Immediatlie bled mutch bluid as ane suir token that ye was the author of his death.

Item ye ar Indyttit and accusit for cuming To William Work in Efaday his hous on Hallowevin four yeiris sene or yr by and knocking at his door They wold not let yow in nor geve yow lodgeing Quha depairting murmuring and miscontent his wyff pairtit with child upon the morne.

Item ye are Indyttit and accusit for that in bear seid tyme the last yeire ye cuming to Johne Spence in Uppettoun his hous and the said Johns Wyff being calling ane calff to the grass ye cam in and was angrie that sho sould have called out the calff quhen ye com in and turneing yow twys about on the floor ye went out and Immediatlie the calff being ane yeir old took seiknes and deit be your witchcraft and sorcerie.
Item ye ar Indyttit and accusit for that on Santt Thomas evin four yeiris sene or yr by ye cuming to Williame Scott in Poldrit his hous and knocking thrie severall tymes at the doore

and ane hour betwix every tyme and ye not gettin in went away murmuring. Thrie dayes efter the guid wyff becam mad and four beastis deit the same yeir and ane ox fell over the craig and deit of the fall.

Item ye ar Indyttit and accusit for that on Candlmesevin fyve yeiris sene ye cam to Gilbert Sandie in Isbister his hous and saught ane plack of silver in almis fra him for his mearis that they might be weill over the yeir, as ye said David Henrie haid done that day, Quha said to yow that he haid nather silver corne nor meall to spair bot baid his wyff geve yow thrie or four stokis of kaill and bene gane away The said Gilbertis wyff followed yow with the kaill but ye wold not tak thame. And upoun the second day efter his best hors standing on the floor becam wood and felled himself and deit and the thrid night thairefter his best meir deit.

Item ye ar Indyttit and accusit for cuming to the said Gilber-tis hous in spring tyme last and the said Gilbertis wyff wald not let yow in, and ye going away took the proffeit of hir milk be your witchcraft and sorcerie.

Item ye ar Indyttit and accusit for yt ye cam to Johne Bewis hous in Waa tua yeiris sene and sought almiss and got nane, and ye said he sould repent it, and about noone his best kow haveing fallen in ane myre and tane out be him his wyff and servands sho wald not stand, and ye cuming thair put thrie earis of bear having first spit on thame, in the kowis mouth and said to them that cam to bear hir home that they neidit not mak yt travell and ane littell quhyll efter the kow being al-most dead and not able to draw ane foot to hir, rais with [out] help and gaid home be your witchcraft and devilrie.

Item ye ar Indyttit and accusit for that fyve or sex yeiris sene, ye cam to David Quoynameikill his fathers hous at the making of his yull banket and got almis and yt they wold not sufferre yow to abid all night qlk ye tald to Margaret Alebuster that they refusit yow ludging and said it was guid to wit if ever the guidman of the hous sould mak ane other Yull bankett and within ffyftene days contractit seikness and deit be yor witchcraft and devilrie.

Item ye are Indyttit and accusit for yt thrie yeiris sene or yr by ye cam to David Quoynameikill motheris hous and got na almis and she being feared that evill sould befall hir as did to otheris befoir night—she fellit hirselff upoun the lintell stane of hir byre and deit within thrie dayes and her servand man also be your witchcraft & devilrie.

Item ye ar Indyttit and accusit for cuming to Michaell Firthis hous in Alebuster in Spring tyme last, and getting no almis becaus the milk was suppit, ye said ye might haue keipit milk to me, and they said they knew not of hir cuming, And the next day efter ane calff deit and now quhen he was convoying yow to Birssay He askit yow at the Slap of Birssay if ye knew anything of the death of his calff ye ansrit haid he not bene so cald to yow nane of your calffis sould not have deit this yeir.

Item ye ar Indyttit and accusit that sex yeiris sene or yr by that Johne Rendall in Brek haid tua calffis lying on the grein and ye askit giff both these calffis wer his and said they wer anew for the first year and ane of the calffis deit befoir nicht be your witchcraft and devilrie.

Item ye are Indyttit and accusit for cuming to Johne Turk in Midland his hous about Witsunday last to get almis and haveing gottin ane drink of new aill ye was not content and befoir ye was tua pair buttis from the hous the aill left working and the said Johne haveing sought yow ane day or tua efter brought yow to his hous againe and took [yow] into his seller and ye spitit amongst the aill and said ye sould warrand him got silver for everie drop of it.

Item ye ar Indyttit and accusit for yt aucht yeiris sene ye hanting to Andro Matches hous in Sundiehous, he wantit the proffeit of his milk and having complenit To Sir Johne Buchanan Shreff for the tyme of how ye met the said Andro upoun the morne and said he sould repent yesterdayes work and the same day ane ox Strick of his deit and about thrie quarteris of ane year efter The said Andro haveing cum to Evie to the Session of the Kirk to complene of yow, ye met with him thrie dayes efter and said to him He was always dealling with you and complening yow and and yt he sould repent it, And thrie dayes efter the said Andro becam mad and ye being send for, and how shoone ye cam to his hous he becam better and fell on sleip and quhen ye haid gottin meat befoir ye teastit it ye spat thrys over your left shulder and the said Androis wyff fearing ye haid bene doing moir evill strak yow, and ye said let me alone for yor guidman wilbe weill.

Item ye ar Indyttit and accusit for yt four yeiris sene ye cam to Manss Quoynameikills hous and soucht almis and got nane at yt tyme, Bot his mother haveing promeised to geve yow

71

milk qwhen hir kow calved ye cam againe that same day the kow calved and soucht almis bot she wald geve yow nane, And ye said ye put me ay of, geve me yt ye promeised me for now your kow is calved and said she sould have ather mair or less milk or ye cam againe and about aucht days efter the kow deit, be your witchcraft & devilrie.

Item ye ar Indyttit and accusit for yt at alhallowmes bygane ane yeir ye cam to the said Manss and sought ane peice colop quha wald geve you nane and ye said befoir ye cam againe he sould have colopis to geve and within ffourtene dayes efter his best ox deit be yor witchcraft & devilrie.

Item ye ar Indyttit and accusit for yt in winter last ye cam to the sd Manss hous and sought ait meall, and he refusand yow, ye said he sould have mair or less or ye cam againe and four-tene dayes efter his kill with aittis took fyre & brunt be your witchcraft & devilrie.

Item ye ar Indyttit and accusit for yt of your awne confessioun efter ye met your Walliman upoun the hill ye cam to Wil-liame Rendalls hous quha haid ane seik hors and promeised to haill him if he could geve yow tua penneys for everie foot, And haveing gottin the silver ye hailled the hors be praying to your Walliman, Lykeas ye have confest that thair is nather man nor beast sick that is not tane away be the hand of God bot for almis ye ar able to cur it be praying to your Walliman, and yt thair is nane yt geves yow almis bot they will thryve ather be sea or land if ye pray to yor Walliman.
And generallie ye the said Jonet Rendall alias Rigga ar In-dyttit and accusit for airt & pairt of the said abominable su-perstitioun and superstitious abuseing and disceaveing of

the people and in useing and practeising of witchcraft and sorcerie and in gevin yor selff furth to have sutche craft and knawledge thairby abusing the people and sua reput & halden. And yr foir and for the pointis of dittay committit be yow In maner above writtin aucht and sould underly the law and be adjudgit to the death for the same and In example of otheris to do the lyk And yor guids and gear esheit & Inbroucht to his majesties use conforme to the act of p'liament and comon law and daylie practeis observit in sick caissis.

CURIA VICECOMITATUS et JUSTICIARIÆ de ORKNEY et ZETLAND tenta apud Birssay in aula ibid., per honorabilem virum magistrum Joannem Dick vicecomitem et Justiciarium deputat dict. vicecomitatus undecimo die mensis Novembris 1629.

Curia legitime affirmata.

The qlk day the sd sheref deput chusit Mr Harie Aitkin in[terim] Clerk, Rob. Scollay in. procuratour fishall, Thomas Young in. Officer.

Compeirit Wm Scollay procuratour fishall and producit the dittayes desyring thame to be red and the pannell accusit yrupoun.

The pannell present confest that Walliman cam to hir first in Nicoll Jockis hous in Halkland and sho maining yt sho was poor and haid nothing. He said to hir yt sho sould leive be almiss and that thair was nather man nor beast seik that wer not dead lie be the hand of God bot she getting almiss and praying to Walliman he wald haill thame, and if she got no almiss he wald be angrie and mak thair beastis die.

Confest the second point of dittay anent Manss Works wyff that sho sd sho sould repent it and yt Walliman gared the kow fall over the craig, and eft. sho was reprovit yt Walliman gared the sd Manss wyff die.

Confest the thrid point that the corne sho got was bot shillingis and yt sho was not content and yt Walliman slew the meiris and the man and as he promeised he was trew to hir.

Confest the fourt point that sho was miscontent that Wm Work wald not geve hir lodging and yt Walliman was angrie at it and gared his wyff pairt with chyld.

Confest the fyft point and yt Walliman gared the calff die.

Confest the sext point that they wold not let hir in and got na almiss and Walliman was angrie at it and gared his wyff run mad and the beast die.

Confest the sevent point yt Gilbert Sandie wald geve hir nothing and yt Walliman wrought conforme to the dittay.

Confest the aucht point and yt Walliman took away the proffeit of the ky.

Confest the nynt point yt sho put bear in the kowis mouth bot dennyis sho spat on it.

Confest the tent point yt sho sd to Mart Alebuster conforme to the dittay, and yt Walliman keipit promeis.

Confest the ellevint point that sho got no almiss fra David Quoynameikills wyff.

Confest the twelff point anent the calffis that sho got na almiss and giff they deit Walliman did it.

Confest the threttin point anent John Turk's aill that it was bot little she got and yr foir Walliman took away the proffeit of it.

Confest the ffourtene point anent Andro Matchis.

Confest the fyftene point anent Manss Quoynameikills wyff and yt sho sould have ather mair or less milk or she cam againe becaus sho got na almiss.

Denyit the sextene point anent Manss quoynameikills ox.
Denyit the sevintene point.
Confest the hailling of Wm Rendalls horss.
Confest the rest of yt point of dittay.
Dennyit the generall.
The pfishall desyrit that the pannell myt be put to the tryell of ane assyss.

The pannell present could alege nothing in the contrair.
Assisa.
[Fourteen names given.]

That the assyss was laufulie sworne and admittit but objection of the pannell. The pfishall askit actis and protestit for error.

The procuratour fishall producit Manss Inerair, Manss Work, Wm. Work, Jon. Spence, Wm. Scottie, Gilbert Sandie, Jon. Sandie, Manss Wood, David Quoynameikill, Michaell Firth, Jon. Turk, Alexr Matches, Andro Matches, and Manss Quoynameikill in witnesses.

The Assyss passing out of Judgment chusit Hew Halcro chancelar.

Manss Wood and Gilbert Sandie deponed yt they wer send for to bear home the kow bot Jonet Rigga was cuming fra the kow befoir they cam yr.

Michaell Firth in Alebuster deponed yt quhen he was cuming to Birssay with hir out of the slap sho confest to him conforme to the dittay that if he haid geven hir almiss his calff haid not deit.

Andro Matches depones that sho spak these words conforme to his point of dittay and that these thingis befell him.

Manss Quoynameikill depones anent the ox that sho said he sould have colopis anew to geve befoir sho cam againe and yt he sould have ather moir or less ait maill or she cam againe and yt the event followit conforme to hir words and dittay bot will not tak it upoun his conscience yt she did it.

The assyss reenterit and in Judgment all in ane voice be the mouth of the chanr. ffyles the pannell of the haill speciall pointis of dittay conforme to hir confessioun, and in the twelff fourtene and sextene pointis conforme to the probatioun And in the generall that sho was ane disceaver of the people and gave hirselff furth to have knawledge to do evill, and if ever she promeised evill, evill befell, and reput the haldin ane common witch. And remittis sentence to the Judge and dome to the Dempster. HEW HALCRO.

The Judge acceptis the determinatioun of the assyss and ordaines the pannell to be tane be the lockman and convoyed to the place of executioun with hir hands bund behind hir bak and worriet at ane stoup to the dead and brunt in assis. Qlk Robert Sinclair dempster in Birssay benorth gave for dome.

From a note-book of the late George Petrie, Sheriff Clerk of Orkney, preserved in the library of Society of Antiquaries of Scotland, Edinburgh.

Orkney. *Trial of Elspeth Reoch,* 1616.—Curia Justiciariæ Vicecomitatus de Orknay tenta apud Kirkwall in nova domo prope Palatium de Yeardis ibidem per honorabilem virum Henricum Stewart de Carlougie Justiciarum ac Vicecomitem deputatum dicti Vicecomitatus die duodecimo Martii 1616.

Curia tenta et legitime affirmata.

The quhilk day anent the dittay criminall gevin in and persewit at the instance of Robert Coltart procurator fiscal of the said sheriffdom Aganes Elspeth Reoch dochter to umquhill Donald sumtyme pyper to the Earl Reoch of Cathnes ffor certane poyntis of dittay of witchcraft underwritten That is to say In the first for airt part using committing and practising of the abominable and divilesch cryme of witchcraft in giveing ear and credite to the Illusiounes of the Devell Quhairby scho fenyeit hirselff dumb And illudit and deceaveit his Majesteis subjectis in maner underwritten viz In the first for that sho confest that quhen shoe wes ane young las of tuelf yeiris of age or therby and haid wandereit out of Cathnes quher sho wes borne to Lochquhaber ye cam to Allane McKeldowies wyfe quha wes your ant And haveing remaneit with her be the space of aucht weekes quho duelt with hir husband in a Loch That she upon ane day being out of the loch in the contrey and returning and being at the Loch syd awaiting quhen the boit sould fetch hir in That thair cam tua men to her ane cled in blak and the uther with ane grein tartane plaid about him And that the man with the plaid said to her she wes ane prettie And he wald lerne her to ken and sie ony thing she wald desyre The uther man said she wald nocht keep counsell and foirbaid him He ansuerit he wald warrand hir And she being desyrous to knaw said how could she ken that And he said Tak ane eg and rost it And tak the sweit of it thre Sondayis And with onwashin handis wash her eyes quhairby she sould sie and knaw ony thing she desyrit And to persuade hir he directit her to ane aunttis hous of hir awin quha wes ane widow that haid ane oy that wes with chyld to ane uther wyffis husband on-knawen to ony And quhen she cam she sould luik in hir face and tell hir she is with bairne to ane uther wyfes husband And sa within a short space therefter going to hir Aunttis hous how sone she saw the young woman she said she wes with bairne as the man had said to hir And shoe denying said to hir she wald repent it within a short space Thairefter the young woman considering that she knew hir estait desyrit sum cure at hir that she micht part with bairne Quha ansuerit she could give her nane Bot remembering that she wes cum in to Allane McKeldowies hous that day that the tua men came to hir That he haveing speirit at her quhat men thois wer that wer with hir at the Loch syd And quhat they haid said to hir And she denying he foirbaid you to fear For they wer freindis of his quha wald do hir no hurt And that he knew quhat they said to hir So she remembring that Allane had skill she said to the young woman that he wald help hir Quher-upoun she and she gaid together to the Loch And spak with him quha refusit to give hir onything to slay the bairne And thairefter within tua yeir she bure her first bairne quhilk wes gottin be ane James Mitchaell at the Kirk of Murthlie upoun Spey within Balveny And being delyverit in hir sisteris hous the blak man cam to her that first came to hir at Lochquhaber And callit him selff ane farie man quha wes sumtyme her kinsman callit Johne Stewart quha wes slane be Mc Ky at the doun going of the soone And therfor nather deid nor leiving bot wald ever go betuix the heaven and the earth quha delt with you tua nychtis and wald never let her sleip persuading hir to let him ly with hir wald give you a guidly fe And to be dum for haveing teacheit her to sie and ken olny thing she desyrit He said that gif she spak gentlemen wald trouble hir and gar hir give reassounes for hir doings Quhairupoun she mycht be challengeit and hurt And upoun the thrid nycht that he com to hir she being asleip and laid his hand upoun hir breist and walkint her And thairefter semeit to ly with her And upoun the morrow she haid no power of hir toung nor could nocht speik quhairthrow hir brother dang hir with ane branks quhill she bled becaus she wald nocht speik and pat ane bow string about hir head to gar her speik And thairefter tuik her three severall tymes Sondayis to the kirk and prayit for hir Fra the quhilk tyme she still continewit dumb going about and deceaveing the people Synding telling and foir shawing thame quhat they had done and quhat they sould do And that be the secund sicht grantit to hir in maner foirsaid She saw Robert Stewart sone naturall to umquhill Patrik sumtyme earl of Orkney with Patrik Traill to quhom she was with bairne and certane utheris with towis about thair craigis in Edmond Callendaris hous at ther efternoones drink befoir the Earl of Caithnes cuming to the cuntrey And that be plucking of the herb callit Merefow quhilk causis the nose bleid He haid taucht hir to tell quhatsover sould be speirit at hir Be sitting on hir rycht knie and pulling and pilling it betwix hir mid finger and thumb And saying of In nomine patris filii et spiritus sancti be vertue quherof sche haweit ane bairne to Magnus Sinclair in Sorne at the desyre of his wyf At quhilk tyme on yule day she confest the devell quhilk she callis the farie man lay with hir At quhilk tyme he bade hir leave Orkney and go home to her awin contrey becaus this countrey was Priestgone quhilk he exponit that ther wes our mony Ministeris in it And gif she taryit she wald be hurt And forder for airt part useing hanting and conversing with the Devell at diverse and sindrie tymes and at severall partis &c &c as at mair lenth is contenit in the saidis dittayis The lenth is contenit in the saidis dittayis The said procuratour fiscali being personally present and the said defendar being lykwayis personalie present quha enterit on pannall haveing no lawfull caus quhy she sould nocht pas to the knawledge of ane assyse Quhairupoun the procuratour fiscali desyring the dittay is to be put to the knawledge of ane assyse and the pannall to be accusit therupoun Efter accusatioun the said Elspeth confest the haill poyntis of dittay abonewrittin And therfor the Judg remittit the dittayis to the knawledge of ane assyse quham he ordanit to be callit.

Nomina Assisæ.
[Sixteen names given.]

Quhilk persones of assyse being reccavit admittit and sworne but lawfull objectioun of the pannall and removeit out of Judgement nominat and ellectit William Bannatyne of Gairsay chancellar And efter dew deliberatioun haid anent the dittayis produceit and haill poyntis therof And reentering on judgement agane the haill assyse be the mouth of the said chancellar fyllit the said Elspeth of the haill poyntis of dittay abonespecifeit And remittit sentence to the Judge and dome to the Dempster Quhilk deliberatioun the Judge than present acceptit And decernit and ordanit the said Elspeth Reoch to be tane be the lockmane to the place of executioun betuix and thrie efter none and to be wirryet at ane staik quhill she be deid And therefter to be burnt in assis Quhilk the Dempster gave for dome.   —Maitland Club Miscellany, pp. 187-191.

Sanday, Orkney. *Trial of Marrione Richart,* 1633.—Examination of the Charges of Witchcraft and Sorcery against Marrione Richart or Layland before the Kirk-Session of Sanday.

The Dittayis giwen in to our Sessioun off Sanday, the 17 day of March, Imvic and threttie and thrie zeiris [1633] wpon

Marrione Richart [or] Layland, of Wichcraft.

The quhilk day, annent the tryell of James Fischer, the said Marrione's oy, that quhair the said James Fischer confessit and told, befoir the sessioun, that wpon ane sax or sevin zeir since, that the said James being keiping Magnus Smyth his suyne, and going wpe along ane old house callit the House of Howing Greinay, the quhilk old howse being standing woyd and weast, and the wather being cold and stormie, the said James went in to the said old house to flee from ane cold schowr; and quhen he cam in to the old house, he saw the said Marrioun, his guiddame, siting within the fornameit old howse, accompanied with Cattrein Miller; and deponit that he did sie ane blak man siting betwixt the said Catrein and the said Marrione; and deponit, that the said Catrein cryit fearcelie, Cause take him, for he will tell wpon ws. The said Marrioun ansuerit and said, Let him allone, for he will not be beleiwit. Item, it is deponed be Margrett Smieton, spous to James Fell, that that night that ye wer in the stockis, Catherine Miller said to Marioun Layland, The pleague of God wpon thy oy, for gif yea had done that quhilk I bad ye, he hadd nott beine trowbling ws now.

Lykwayis, the said Marrioun Layland did wasch the feit of James Dauidsones cat into his bait water, becaus he could not get no fisch that zeir, thinking thairby and saying, that the said James in tyme comming wold get more fisch in respect off hir work in wasching off the catis feit into his bait watter; and quhen scho had waschin the cat thairin, did take the water quheirin the cat was waschin, and did cast it after him quhen he did go to the sea.

Lykewayis, the xxiiij day of March, Magnus Smyth deponit, that the boy presentlie wpone the morning therafter told the said Magnus that he did sie the dewill, and told him the quhilk faschioun. Lykwayes, the same day Dauid Jock and his wyff tryitt and confessit that wpon fyve or sax zeir since, that the said Marrioun cam to the said Dauid Jok his house, and the said Dauid was going to the sea, and was making mone that he had not luck to get fisch that zeir: The said Marrioun ansuerit and said, that that might be eassillie mendit, and callit for the thing that geid about the fyre, quhilk was the cat, and said that scho wold wasch the cat his head and feit into the watter quherin the bait was to be keipit, and said that scho wold take that watter and cast itt about him and wpon him, and into his sea caschie, and into his bait coubbie, and quhen he cam to the sea he schould get fisch.

Farther, it is deponit be Margret and Elspet Sandisones, that the said Elspet vpon fyue or sax zeir since, contrakit ane deadlie disease, in so farre that scho was senceles and myndles for ane long speace; the said Marrione cam to the said Elspetis house, and made ane watter, quhilk schocallis ane remeddie for forspeaking; the said Marrioun tuik watter into ane round coupe, and went out into the byre, and tuik sumthing out off hir pursse, like wnto great salt, and did put it into the watter, and did spit thrie severall tymes into the watter; and scho confesit hir selff quhen scho had done so, scho aundit in bitt, quhilk is ane Nourne terme, and to exponit into right languag, is alse mikill as scho did blew hir breath thairin, and sent it in to the woman, with the servant woman off the house, and directit that the woman should be waschin hand and face thairin, and scho should be restorit to hir health againe. This the said Marrioun confesit befoir the sessioun; and it is grantit be the woman that the watter was made wnto, that the said Marrioun said wnto the lass, that iff ewer the lass reueillit it againe scho should never thryue, and so schune after that the lass reueillit the wordis, scho deit.

Quhilk day it is confest be Robert Drewer and his wyff, that threttein zeir since, the said Marrioun and Robert Drewer was duelling both at ane house and ane biging; that thair was ane powr woman that was trauelling of chyld in the said Marriones house, and desyrit ane soupe off milk from the said Marrioun, quhilk in no wayis the said Marrioun wold grant, the powre woman sent in to the said Robertis house and got ane soup off milk from his wyff, and immediatlie thairefter the said Robert his wyff lossit hir proffit of hir haill milk; quhairfor the said Robert Dreweris wyff cam in to the said Marrioun Layland, and did lament for her profeit that scho wantit. The said Marrioun ansuerit the woman and said, Goe thy way to the sea, and tell nyne beares off the sea come in, that is to say, nyne waues off the watter, and let ane off the nyne goe back againe; and the nixt thair thairafter take thrie luiffullis off that watter, and put within thy stowpe, and quhen thou comes heame put it within thy kirne, and thow will get thy profeit agane.

The last day of March.

Compeirit Helin Hamiltoun, spouse to James Keith, and

deponit, that scho and hir haill fammillie was straitit with drouth for the space off xx dayis ore ane mounth, that no drink could quench thar dreuth; quhairfor the said Helin and her husband alledgit the said Marrioun for the great thrist that thay had. Wpon ane Sunday the said Marrioun cam to the said Helins house, and had ane muchkin off small-aill with hir into ane chapping can, and offerit it to the said Heline and hir famillic to drink; and the said Helin refusit to drink it, bot the said Marrion wrgit it more and more vpon hir, and said that scho had ane sonsie hand and hir mother befoir hir day, and made euerie ane off them to drink thairoff; and immediatlie thairafter thair thrist was easit, and the heauie wycht that was wpon them was easit during the time of their thrist and dreuth.

The samen day, Williame Fothringhame, benorth, deponit be him, that the said Marrioun cam to his house to get almis, and his wyff not being at leasur to giwe her almis, scho went to the dore, and did say, going to the dore, that scho should losse aise mikill schortlie; and aucht dayis after that his best cow diet.

Quhilk day, deletit by Margret Thomsone spouse to James Rolosay, to James Cok in Lopnes, Nicoll King and Magnus Skea, quhilk are thrie elderis off our sessioun, that the said Marrioun cam to Stronsay, to the said Margretis house, and the said Margret had nyne ky quhilk was not riddin; and scho said to hir, Giwe me almis, and befoir this day fyftein dayis ilk kow in zour aucht sall be riddin; quhilk almis scho gave hir, and befoir that day aught dayis, ilk kow that scho had was riddin.

The 7 day off Appryll 1633.

Quhilk day, annent the dittayis of Wichcraft given in to the sessioun, when Catrein Miller compeirit, Hew Peace and Wrsalay Fea, his spouse, and deponit, that wpon ane sax zeir since, that the said Vrsalay wantit the profeit off hir milk, and the said Wrsalay sent hir servant woman and milkit the said Cattrein Milleris kow, and did put it into her kirne; and immediatlie quhen scho kirnit the milk, scho got ix markis butter, quhair befoir, off alse mikill milk, alse mony dayis milk, alse mony mealtitis off milk, during the time that scho wantit hir profit, did not get bot tua markis butter; and quhen scho had the best, scho got not bot tua markis butter ay and quhill that scho got the milk off her cow; and four and xx houris after the said Wrsalay contrakit ane deadlie disease, quhilk contenint for the space of sax weikis; and at the end off the sax weikis, the said Marrione cam to the said Wrsalay and desyrit ane drink off milk from the kirne, and said iff scho got it scho should get hir health, and scho gave hir ane drink off milk, and scho was presentlie better off hir disease, and losit the profit off hir milk, and wantis it as zitt.

Farther deponit, be Margaret Orrok, laughfull daughter to William Orrock, that the said William had ane horse quhilk was seik; the said Catrein bad the said Margret get thrie sundrie sortis off fillneris, and put them within ane siwe, and sift them ouer the bak of the horse quhilk was seik, and he wold be haill.

The 14 day off Appryll 1633.

Deponit be Barbaray Sinclair, spouse to the said William Orrock, that scho had ane kow that was standing haill in to the byre, and the said Catrein cam in to the said Barbarayis house to puik sum bair, and presentlie the kow fell seik; quhen scho geid away with the corne that scho was knoking, and that word did rys that the cow was seik, the said Catrein cam to the house; and quhen scho cam in and sau the cow, scho was restorit to health agane, and did eat hir meat weill enugh.

The 19 day off Appryll.

Deponit be Margret Browne, spouse to William Flet, that quhair the said Margret discordit with Catreine Miller, the said Margret contrakit ane deadlie diseas; and scho said to the said Margret, "evill might thow put the yeir aff the;" thairafter scho contrakit ane senslesnes quilk continuit for the space of ane halff yeir; and at the halff yeiris end, the said Margret cam to hir, and the said Catrein tuik her by the hand, and immediatlie got hir health, and ay since was weill.

The samen day compeirit Catrein Sowents, and deponit befoir the sessioune, that the said Catrine Miller wrongit hir, in respect that scho faund fault with hir, becaus scho did take keall out off hir maisteris yaird, and hir daughter did tak keall out off the yaird, and did goe heome to Catrine Milleris house with the keall, and told hir mother that the said Kaitrine Souanes fand fault with hir for takeing away of the keall; the said Catrine Miller sent hir daughter bak to the house with the keall, and did cast the keall upon the said Catrine Sowenes breist, being nurisch to John Browne in the tyme, and presentlie scho losit hir milk for the speace of xiiij dayis; and at the isschow off the xiiij dayis, the said Catrine Miller cam to the house quhair the nurisch was, and told the guidwyff off the house that scho had dreamit, that iff scho wold giwe hir daughter almis, the nurisch showld get hir milk againe; and quhen scho got almis, scho get hir milk againe also weill as it was befoir.

The samen day compeirit Dauid Peace, and deponit, that the said Catrine Miller had ane sone keiping his ky, and bccaus that he did put away the boy from the ky, scho said that he should rew it, and immediatlie ane off the ky dieit, and schort after, the rest dieit also.

The 21 day off Appryll.

Deponit be James Fea, bailzie, that the said Catrine Miller had ane sone keiping Johne Broune his ky and guidis, and the boy was put from the guidis; and scho did curse and pray ewill for the guidis, and therefter the most pairt of them dieit, and the rest that liewit did neuer guid, nor zit yield milk, since the boy ged from them. Farther, it is deponit be Wrsalay Fea, that the said Catrein Miller cam into Hew Peace hir husbandis house, and did pray ewill for Jon Brounes guidis, and said, "God, let his guidis newer thryue better nor hir sone did."

Quhilk day deponit be Jennet Fothringham, spouse to John Peace, younger, that quhair the said Jennet was angrie with hir for comming so earlie ilk moirning to hir guidmotheris house befoir the sone ryseing, presentlie the said Jennet falis in to ane extraordinarie diseas, so that scho might not goe out off hir guidmotheris house in to hir awin house, quhilk was both closse togidder, bot did creip wpon handis and feit quhill scho cam to hir bed; and the said Catrine cam in to hir and did lay hir hand upon hir head, and did cause give hir ane sowpe off milk, and scho grew also weill and in also guid health as ewer scho was befoir; and all this was dune within the speace of tua houris.

Farther deponit be Williame Roy, elder, that the said Williame discordit with hir, and scho did strik him upon the back, betuixt the shoulderis, with hir hand, and presentlie the power off his body was takin away, in so farre that he could not no duetie off ane man touardis his wyff, quhair tua nightis befoir he was alse apt and abili for his wyff as ever he was befoir; and never since the discord was weill as he should be.

Abbotsford Club Miscellany, pp. 150-156.

[In the record of her trial which follows her examination the same charges are produced against her with the addition of the following.]

Attour, ye are indyted and accuised for airt and part of the said abominable superstition, in that ye cam to Stronsay about tua or three yeires since, in simer, and asking almis fra Andro Couper, skipper of ane bark, he said to yow, "Away, wich, carling, devil, a farthing ye noll fa"; quhairvpoun ye departed very offendit, and incontinently he going to sie, the bark being vnder saill, he ran mad, and wold have luppin over burd, an his sone seing him, gat him in his armes, and held; quhervpon the seiknes imediatly left him, and his sone ran mad; and Thomas Patersone seing him tak the madness, and the father to turne weill, ane dog being in the bark, took the dogg and bledded him vpon the sone his shoulders, and therafter keist the said dog mad, quhairby these in the bark wer saifed; quhilk being done, all the doggers at the sch[ore] . . . [torn in MS.] landlyeris for feir gaue yow abundantly; quhilk all wes done be your witchcraft and [divelrie]: Quhilk ye cannot deny.

[She was sentenced to be worried at a stake and afterwards burnt to ashes.]

[On the back of the dittay against Marion Richart mention is made of a woman "that took girss and baik a bannok, and give it to the goodman of Papa his grieve, quba deit; and the dog that got the bannok deit. The bannok wes for keiping thair profite."

"Elen Forster can mend baith the heartcake and beanschaw, and put down horss to the goodman of Langskaill."]

Abbotsford Club Miscellany, pp. 161, 163.

Orkney. *Trial of Agnes Scottie*, 1616.—Agnes Scottie was charged "with committing and practiseing the devilishe and abominable cryme of witchcraft in that she, vpoun ane Sonday befoir the sone rysing, about fastings-evin, came to ane wall besyde James Corrigillis hous, and thair wasch[ed] hir face and certane partis of her claythis; and Robert Gadie persaveing hir, quha wes servant to the said James, contractit presentlie ane trembling and shuddering in his flesh, tuik seiknes, and thairefter dyit. . . . Item, for that seven yeiris syne or thairby, sche haveing discordit with vmquhill William Tailzeouris sister, quha comin to reprove hir for hir evill speiches aganes hir sister, in quhais face she spat, being on a Sonday,—the said William immediatlie thairefter conceaveit a great fear and trembling in his flesch, contractit seiknes, and dyit on Weddinsday thairefter. Item, for that Nicoll Smyth havein takin ane cottage fra the gudman of Brek, quhilk wes in hir possession, and haveing transportit his cornes thair, she cam about hallowmes, being washing hir claithes, and laid thame on his corne, and nocht on hir awin, and set ane cog full of watter in the said Nicollis way, quha in the cuming by cust ouir the samen, thairefter contractit ane great seiknes. His vmquhill master, callit Mans Matthes, cumand to reprove hir for his manes seiknes, efter she haid tuckit him and given him mony injurious wordis, he conceaveit ane great fear and trembling, contractit seiknes, and within sevin day is thairefter dyit." —ROGERS, vol. iii. p. 298.

Amidst various suspicious proceedings, wherein washing herself and her clothes were included, she "past the boundis of hir ground, and thair sat doun plaiting hir feit betuix the merchis." —DALYELL, p. 448.

Trial of William Scottie, vagabound, warloche, 1643.—A cow being drawn out of the byre as dead, William Scottie "straikit the kow along the head, and then drew his hand vpoun the cattis head, and shoe fell dead." *Ibid.*, p. 109.

He put his hand on the sufferer's "sore syd, and after vpone the hearth stone," which cured her in an hour. *Ibid.*, p. 125.

Coming to William Okilsetters, he "yeid about his hous twys or thrys witherwardis: and again, he being in Patrick Gareochis hous, yeid and cum witherwardis about the William's hous back againe: that same night, befoir day sett, the said William Ockilsetteris wyf fell deadlie seik, and tint hir milk that shoe had in abundance befoir, and continewit seik quhill he laid his hand vpoun hir: and incontinentlie shoe gat hir health, and the young mear foill, that was standing vpoun the hous floore, took seikness, and did byt the stones untill shoe died presentlie." *Ibid.,* p. 459.

Trial of Isobel Sinclair, 1633.—It was alleged against her, that during seven years, "sex times at the reathes of the year, shoe hath bein controlled with the Phairie; and that be thame, shoe hath the second sight: quhairby shoe will know giff thair be any fey bodie in the hous." *Ibid.,* p. 470.

To preserve cattle she directed people to "fyre ane piece of linying cleath, and sing ane hair of the beast at alhalow even." —*Ibid.,* p. 193.

Trial of John Sinclair, 1633.—"Vnder silence and clud of nycht, Imvic. ten [1610] years," he carried his distempered sister along with him: "he horsed her backward from quhair scho lay, to the Kirk of Hoy, quhair he met the kirk sevin faddome; at quhat tyme ane voyce appeirit saying, 'sevin is ower many for ane syne.' Thairefter, he tuik hir, and layed hir at the north syd of . . . be directioun of the devill: And in the morning, the first thing scho saw, was ane boit with fyve men, quhairof four perischit, and ane was saiff—be the quhilk divellrie the woman becam weill." The wonted test which betrayed so many, denoted that the culprit had accomplished this sacrifice to redeem his sister; for, when accused of the foul fact, "after the dead men wer found, and forcit to lay his handis vpoun thame, they gushit out with bluid and watter at mouth and noise." —*Ibid.,* pp. 179–80.

Trial of Bessie Skebister, 1633.—She was accused of acting thus towards Margaret Mudic, whose cow trespassed among her corn. "Ye sat doun, and taking of your curtch, sheuk your hair lous, and ever since shoe has bein so vehementlie pained, that shoe dwins and becoms wors and wors: and hes nevir bein weill since ye curst hir, or sheuk your hair lous." The jury convicted her of "taking of hir curtch, shaking of hir hair [lous], and Margaret Mudie's diseas."   —*Ibid.,* p. 451.

It was also alleged against her that James Sandieson, under a severe distemper, affirmed, "that in his sleip, and oftymes waking he was tormented with yow, Bessie, and vther twa with yow, quhom he knew not, cairying him to the sea, and to the fyre, to Norroway, Yetland, and to the south—that ye had ridden all thes wayes with ane brydle in his mouth."
                                    —*Ibid.,* p. 591.

At Sowlis Skerrie, on a certain day, it was alleged against her that "James Chalmers came to yow, and finding yow weiping for the boittis, he said to yow, all is not weill if ye be weiping: ye answerit, ye weipit for the truble they wer in, but not for their death, for they wold come home. It was replyit to yow, be the said James, they culd not be saife vnles they went be north the cuntrey: ye answerit, that ye suld warrand they suld not goe about the cuntrey; but that they suld come home that same way they yeid, quhilk cam to pas as ye spak." Another boat being driven out to sea, and one of the oars cast ashore on the Isle of Wais, "the gudwyff of the Bow, having hir eldest sone vpoun the boat, send on of hir servands to speir at yow giff the boat was weill." She answered, "goe your way home, for they ar all weill, and will be home or they sleep: and so it was that they came home that same nicht." *Ibid.*, p. 474

The particular side of a coin dropped into water proved the health of an absent friend. If "the cross of the sexpence be vp, then they are weill; gif not, they are not weill."—*Ibid.*, p. 512.

Hay, Orkney. Elspet Smith, a witch, 1672.—With respect to taking away the strength of ale they give the witch the same power, as the curious reader may see by the following extract from an old Session Register of Hay:—"4th August, 1672.—After preaching sedr. the minr. and elders This day compeared Elspet Smith and gave in a complaint upon Mareon Mangie for slandering her as guilty of witchcraft, in saying that the said Elspet Smith complainer, by sending for ane pynt of aill from the said Mereon selling the same, Did thereby take awa the fruit and fusion of ane dusson of pynts or thereby that remained in the vessel &c." —LOW, p. 6 note.

Shetland. Helen Stewart, a witch.—In Shetland a few years agoe, a Judge having condemned an old Woman and her daughter called Helen Stewart for Witchcraft, sent them to be burn'd. The Maid was so stupid, that she was thought to be possessed. When she had hung some little time on the Gibbet, a black Pitchy-like ball foamed out of her mouth: and after the fire was kindled, it grew to the bigness of a Walnut, and then flew up like Squibs into the air, which the Judge yet living attests. It was taken to be a visible sign that the Devil was gone out of her.—From "Relation Anent Major Weir," 1684, in SINCLAIR, p. 231.

Orkney. *Trial of Anie Tailzeour, alias Rwna Rowa,* 1624.—
Intrat vpoun pannell, Anie Tailzeour, alias Rwna Rowa, to
vnderly the law befor Sir Johnne Buchanane of Scottiscraig,
Knyght, justice, and schireff-principal of Orknay, at the instance of Robert Chalmer of Ryssay, procuratiour fischall of
the said schireffdome, for certane pointis of Witchcraft, Sorcerie, and Superstitioun, at the least behaueing hir selff to
haue sic skill and knawledge, thairthrow abusing the people
as followis.

In the first, ye the said Anie Tailzeour ar indyttit and accusit
for airt and pairt of the vseing, comitting, and practising
of the diuelische and abhominable cryme of Superstitioun,
Witchcraft, and Sorcerie, in that aucht or nyne yeiris syne,
in fauchland tyme, Williame Burwick in North Ransay, and
William Swanisone thair, being in Airsay, ye came and soght
ane luik beir fra the said William, and Thomas Burwick, sone
to the said William, reprowing your importunitie, ye was angrie, and called him, "gallow bread"! quhilk is, hangit man;
and his father being angrie, baid yow "Away, witch, rigand
theiff!" quhairat ye being angrie, fleat, and chyded, and past
your way. And quhen they yocked the pleuche, the pleuche
wald not enter in the ground, neither for the ane nor the other, temper hir quhat scho wald; and thairefter the culter and
sock gaid out off the pleuche be your witchcraft and diuelrie.

II. Item, ye ar indyttit and accusit for the said cryme of Witchcraft, in that, vpoun the third day of September, Imvjc and
sextene yeiris, ye being wardit be the Sessioun in the Croce
Kirk, Thomas Logie, cuming to his awin hous leat ane evin,
and meitting ane number of cattis within the dyk of Colzigar,

vpoun the brae, among the beir schaues, quhilk vnbesett him, the said Thomas saw your face vpoun ane of [the] cattis; and at the Candlemes thairefter, ye cuming to his hous, and he reproueing yow, alledgand yow to haue bene among the cattis that vnbesett him, ye lughe and skorned it; vpoun the quhilk reprooff, the said Thomas contractit seiknes for the space of tua yeiris, quhill his wyff came to yow, and fleat with yow; and thairefter the said Thomas convalest, and his said wyff immediatlie tuik seiknes, quha yit continwis seik, and not lyk to liue, be your witchcraft and diuelrie.

III. Item, ye ar indyttit and accusit, in that, ane yeir efter, ye cuming to the said Thomas' hous, keipit not the hie gait, but went in through the cornes, and came through his kyne, quha presentlie wanttit thair proffeit for the space of tuentie dayis, and quhen the said Thomas socht yow, and reprowit yow, and boastis to ding yow, that same nycht the proffeit of the kyne was restored, be your witchcraft and diuelrie.

IV. Item, ye ar indyttit and accusit for the forsaid cryme, in that ye, being demandit be Mr Thomas Cok, and Thomas Sinclair, baillie, how ye tuik the proffeit of the kyne and gaue it to vtheris, ye ansuerit, it was to tak thrie hairis of the kowis taill, thrie of her memberis, and thrie of hir papis, and gang thryse woderwardis about the kow, and straik hir in the left syd, and cast the hair in the kirne, and say thryse, "Cum butter, cum," and sua thei sould haue the haill proffeit of that flock, quhair that kow was: Quhilk ye practise be the directioun of the diuell.

V. Item, ye are indyttit and accusit for the cryme forsaid, in that, about mid somer, fyve yeiris syne, James Ego, smyth, his wyff, haueing tane ane loik of your beir, ye said scho sould repent it, and immediatlie ane meir deit to hir worth xx lib.: And becaus scho wald not geue you ane soup milk of ane new callowit kow, ye said so sould scho find it; and presentlie the kow deit: And in winter last, ane foill of the said James, haueing eatten ane schaue of youris, ye prayed God nor the foill burst and beall; quhilk schortlie came to pas, and the foill deit be your witchcraft and deuelrie.

VI. Item, ye ar indyttit and accusit for the cryme forsaid, in that, in Maij Imvjc and auchten, ye being cum to Iver Deirnes hous, ye said that Hew Peace was ane hauey hand vpoun yow, and that he was getting ane quhip for it; and giff he wald not let you alone, he wald get war yit: And the said Hew his wyff being informit thairof, he being diseasit of ane byll, he cam and tuiched the byll, quhairby he was haill within fourtie aucht houris, quhilk, to his opinion, could not have bene in ane quarter of ane yeir, be your witchcraft and diuelrie.

VII. Item, ye ar indyttit and accusit for the said cryme, in that, in November Imvjc and tuentie ane, ye being in Thomas Mure of Quoykankeris hous, ye came to him in the nyght, he being in his bed, and it being ane great storme, and bad him ryse vp and gang about the schoir and he sould find fische; and he being sueir to ryse, ye vrgit him, and said he sould find ane quhaill at the West Bankis, quhilk he did find: Quhilk ye fortald be your witchcraft and divelrie.

VIII. Item, ye ar indyttit and accusit for the said cryme, in that, in haruest thrie yeiris syne, William Spens wyff, haueing refussit you ane schaue of corne, ye tuk the proffeit of his cornes from him and gaue it to his brother, James Spens, be your witchcraft and diuelrie.

IX. Item, ye ar indyttit and accusit for the cryme for-said, in that, in somer thrie yeiris syne or thairby, vpoun our Lady day in haruest, ye came and soght one loik of beir fra William Namlandis wyff, and scho refussing you, ye cast seiknes vpoun hir, quha lay almost ane half yeir; and quhen, be the persuasioun of his dochter, ye cam to his hous, and gaue hir ane piece of bannock to eat, scho presentlie grew haill, be your witchcraft and diuelrie: Quhilk ye cannot deny.

X. Item, ye ar indyttit and accusit for the said cryme, in that, in May last, Mareoun Paulsone, spous to James Fothringhame in Burnes, in Sanday, haueing tane ane luik meall furth of your pock, ye prayed that scho sould suall that eat your meall; quhairvpoun the said Mareoun swalled, and now is dead, be your witchcraft and diuelrie.

XI. Item, ye ar indyttit and accusit for the cryme for-said, in that, fyve yeiris syne or thairby, ye being in Johne Flettis hous, and haueing brocht in some of Annie Peace's peatis, and brunt thame, and scho finding fault with yow, ye said scho sould never burne the rest; and sua thair roise ane great storme that same nyght, and the sea came vp and did wasche all the rest of the peattis away, be your witchcraft and diuelrie.

XII. Item, ye ar indyttit and accusit for the said cryme, in that, efter Yule last, ye being in Robert Ising Millaris hous, in Sanday, and ane lass of his keiping ane bairne, haueing ane luik thrid in hir hand, ye soght the said thrid, and the lass refussit, quha presentlie tuik sick ane franisie, that scho almost cuist the bairne thryse in the fyre, giff scho had not bene stayed; and that the franisie continwit quhill ye gatt the thrid, be your witchcraft and diuelrie.

XIII. Item, in that, efter Yule last, ye haueing cum to the said Robertis mylne, and haueing soght ane luik of meall fra thame that was grinding, and lykwayis fra him selff, and ye being refussit, passing away murmuring and speaking to your selff; the said Robert haueing put on the mylne with the same cornes, quhairof thair was ane pairt grund, for all his skill he could not mak the mylne to gang that day, be your witchcraft and diuelrie.

XIV. Item, ye ar indyttit and accusit for the said cryme, in that ye being broght out of Ethay, be Stevin Tailyeour in Papa Wastray, cam to his hous, and efter aucht dayis haueing soght ane peice butter fra the said Stevin's wyff, and scho refussing yow, vpoun the morne efter, the kow wald not suffer ane to milk hir: And ye being challangit and delaitit to the kirk, and straitlie flightered with ane tedder the tyme of the sessioun, quhen the sessioun raise, ye was standing at the end of the kirk louse, nane being to help yow; and the said Stevin's wyff thairefter incontinentlie contractit seiknes, continwit seik quhil ye came and charmed hir, falddomeing the woman, laying ane hand to hir head, and ane other to hir fute corslingis, saying, "Motheris blissing to the head, motheris blissing to the feit, and motheris blissing to the heart," in plaine scorne; for the wyff continwit seik and deit, be your witchcraft and diuelrie.

XV. Item, ye ar indyttit and accusit, in that, in Junij last, ye being tane to John Chalmeris, officer, ye prayed him to let yow gang or else ye sould rune on the sea and drowne you; and giff he wald keip yow that nyght vndelyght, he sould fische weill, and his kow sould milk weill that yeir.

XVI. And generallie, ye, the said Annie Tailzeour, ar indyttit and accusit as ane comoun witche, for airt and pairt, vseing, committing and practeising of the abhominable cryme of Superstitioun, Witchcraft, and Sorcerie, and in geving your selff furth to have sic craft and knawledge, thairthrow abuseing the people, and wroning and staying man and beast, and sua reput and haldin ane comoun and notorious witche; and thairfor, aucht and sould vndergo the knawledge of ane Assyse, and be adiugit and condemnit to the death, for the caussis forsaidis, in example of vtheris to do the lyk; and your guidis and gear escheit and inbroght to his maiesties vse, conforme to the lawis and daylie practique obseruit in sic caissis.

I. Thomas Burwick maid fayth conforme to the points of the dittay. The pannell denyet.

II. Thomas Logie, present, maid fayth conforme to the dittay to his knawledge.

The pannell denyet.

Lyk as the said Thomas this day deponit and declarit, that scho said, giff he wald get hir out, scho sould do quhat scho could to gar his wyff get hir health, and help hir giff scho myght be helpit.

Jerohme Fothringhame, and Ard Dase, with diuerse vtheris, verefeit the same.

Indifferent anent the vnbesetting of the cattis, and fyllis hir anent his seiknes.

III. The said Thomas maid fayth conforme to the dittay. The pannell denyet. Fyllis.

IV. Mr Thomas Cok confest it is trew. The pannell denyet not, but scho said scho was vncouth, and wist not quhat to say. Fyllis.

V. James Ego, present, maid fayth conforme to the dittay. The pannell denyet. Fyllis.

VI. Hew Peace, present, maid fayth conforme to the dittay. The pannell confest scho tuiched the byll. Fyllis.

VII. The nyghtbouris in Sanday buir it to be trew, and Mr Thomas Muster, present, declarit that Thomas Mure suir in their session, and scho said, giff he reveild it he sould repent it, and that he is continwallie seik sensyne. Fyllis.

VIII. William Spons maid fayth conforme to the dittay. Becaus his brother haid tua mells, and he haid bot four schaves being growing in ane rig. For the corne, ryffis clauso ore. The pannell denyet.

IX. The pannell denyet. Fyllis.

X. The pannell denyet.

Mr Thomas Cok, present, declarit that the said Mareoun, in his presens and John Richartsones, maid fayth that the said Mareoun deponit conforme to the dittay. Fyllis.

XI. The minister declarit that John Flet suir the dittay in presens of the Sessioun. The pannell denyet. Fyllis.

XII. Robert Millar, present, maid fayth conforme to the dittay. The pannell denyet. Fyllis.

XIII. Robert Millar maid fayth conforme to the dittay. The pannell denyet. Fyllis.

XIV. The pannell denyet. Fyllis.

XV. Mr Thomas Cok declarit that he sure it in the Sessioun, The pannell denyet. Fyllis.

XVI. Fyllis.

Curia Justiciariæ, vicecomitatus de Orknay et Zetland, tenta apud Kirkwall in templo Sti. Magni ibidem, per honorabilem Dominum Joannen Buchannane de Scottiscraig, Militem, vicecomitem Principalem eiusdem, et Edwardum Sinclair de Essinquoy, eius Deputatum, decimo quinto die mensis Julij 1624.

The quhilk day compeirit Robert Chalmer, procuratour fischall, and desyrit the dittayis to be put to the knawledge of ane Assyse.

The pannell, present, could alledge no reasonabill caus in the contrair.

ASSISA.
[Fifteen names given.]

That the Assyse was receavit and suorne the procuratour fischall askit instrumentis.

The Assyse, passing out of judgment, nominate James Fea in chanseler:

And reentering againe, the haill Assyse, all in ane voice, Fyllis hir in the haill pointis off dittay aboue writtin, speciali and generall, except the first pairt of Thomas Logeis dittay anent the cattis; and anent William Spens' dittay anent the corne; quhairanent they ryf clauso ore, and remittis sentens to the judge and dome to the dempster. JAMES FEA, Chansseler.

SENTENCE.

The judge ordanis the pannell to be tane be lockman, hir handis bund behind hir bak, and tane be the lokman to the Lonhead, and wirried at ane staik, and brunt in asses: Quhilk Donald Kenner, dempster, gaue for dome.

Abbotsford Club Miscellany, pp. 143-149.

103

Stromness, Orkney. *Trial of Kathrine Taylor.*—Saturday, July last, 1708.—After Prayer Sedr., Minister and elders *pro re nata.*

The said day the minister reported that being informed that Kathrine Brown, spouse to William Stensgar in Southside, had been employing one Kathrine Taylor, a cripple beggar woman in Stromness, to come to her house and wash the said William, who had been long sick and afflicted in his bed, that by her Sorcerie and charming he might come to his health, and that the said Kathrine Brown coming to a common Slap on the high way, carrying the water wherewith the said William was allegit to be washed, in a large Stoup, upon the twenty fourth of June last, about one or two hours in the morning, and emptying the said Stoup in the said Slap: wherefore he had appointed to Summon ye said Kathrine Brown and her Husband to this Dyet. The said Kathrine and her Husband being called compeared, and both of them being accused, denyed the charge, and the said Kathrine stiffly denyed that she had been at the common Slap above written, whereupon the witnesses being called, compeared.

John More son to William More in Yeldabrec of the age of twenty four years, being admitted and deeply sworn purged of malice and partial counsell, deponed; That he saw Kathrine Brown upon the twenty fourth day of June last more than an hour before sunrising, empty a stoup of water in the above mentioned Slap, and he coming to the said Slap did find a Stone and feal on the said water, or where it was spilled and as he was coming near he saw the said Kathrine gather up her coats, and run away most speedily. And that he suspecting some devilrie did break down a slap in another place of the dike and passed over.

George Langskail Deponed, That upon the twenty fourth of June he passed thro' the slap forementioned before sunrising and that he saw water in the said slap, and a little while after his passing the same he was overtaken by bodily indisposition1 tho' he would not blame the said Kathrine Brown therefore.

After several things had passed in the Session we are told That the said Kathrine Brown and her Husband confessed that the said Kathrine Taylor was called and came to their house, and all She did was to say over half a dozen words out of a psalm like a prayer beside the Husband.

The Session appointed Kathrine Taylor to be summoned to answer for using Sorcerie.

Sess. 2d on the same.

Sept. 5, 1708.—Which day compeared Kathrine Taylor in Stromness being summoned to this dyct as were also William Stensgar and Kathrine Brown before mentioned, and the said Kathrine Taylor being accused of alleged Sorcerie and charms—she confessed that Kathrine Brown came for her when she was in Oliver Taylors house in the Southside and told to her her Husbands condition viz., That he wanted the power of one of his Knees, and enquired her if she could not tell out the paine of the said knee. Whereupon the said Kathrine Taylor condescended and went with the said Kathrine Brown to her house, and did tell out the pain of his knee. Being asked by what means she did it, She answered, She laid her hand on his bare Knee and spake these words,

"As I was going by the way, I met the Lord Jesus Christ in the likeness of another man, he asked me what tydings I had to tell and I said I had no tydings to tell, but I am full of pains, and I can neither gang nor stand." "Thou shalt go to the holie kirk, and thou shalt gang it round about, and then sit down upon thy knees, and say thy prayers to the Lord, and then thou shalt be as heall as the hour when Christ was born."

She repeated also the twenty third psalm indistinctlie and declared she did or spake no more. She likewise declared she learned this from an old woman when she was a child; and that she has heard from others that a pain or a stitch has been telled out in that manner, and that she herself has done it before.—Low, pp. 201-203.

Shetland. *Trial of Barbara Thomasdochter, alias Stovd,* 1616.—The "selch bone" with which she stirred her milk to divine the product, "being thereafter cast in the fyir, it crackit and affrayit the hous."   —DALYELL, p. 384.

She told one who churned in vain, that "the lid of hir kirne wald be weit gif she had the profeit of hir milk, and gif it wes dry she wantit it—she wald gif her sum thing gif she wald heild it, that wald do hir guid: and oppnit hir pwrs and tuik ane bone furth therof, quhilk wes the bone of ane manes finger, great at the ane and small at the vther, of twa insh lang or therby, and bad hir steir hir milk with it and she wald get hir profeit: and quhilk bone wes sumquhat bread, and sum hoillis in it, but not throw." After explaining that it was not a human but "ane selch bone" the charmer was convicted of superstitious practices. *Ibid.*, p. 264.

A person named Garth, in Yell, having contracted "ane great fever and lyghtnes in his head, that he could get no rest nor sleip in somer 1613: and Gregorius Thomasone haveing cum to visite him, and informit of the said diseas, he tauld Garth that thair was ane woman in Delting, called Barbara Stovd, quha culd give him ane resting threid." Gregorius repairing to the woman under silence of night, and describing the patient's state, she refused to give him a thread until he should himself apply for it: "quhairof Garth being aduerteisit be the said Gregorius, he come over to hir, and [they] come togither to hir in ane somer morneing, earlie befoir the sone, about Jonesmes 1614: and at said conference, she tuik ane woll threid, and vsit certane crossis and coniurationes vpoun it. She gave it to hir dochter to be given to the said Garth, to be woone about his head nyne nyghtis, and then to be burnt: quhairby Garth gat rest." Afterwards, because, "at certyne tymes of the moone, he found himself not so weel as he wount to be, he came to hir this somer, and desyrit hir to mak him perfyt haill, quhilk she promeisit to do at hallowmes nixt." *Ibid.*, pp. 118, 119.

Orkney. *Trial of Jonet Thomesone, alias Grebok,* 1643.—Helen Languor having quarrelled with Jonet Thomesone, she sickened, and the meat prepared for her became full of worms; but none were seen either in that prepared for her husband or her household. After a donation to the sorceress, she recovered and worms were seen no more. *Ibid.*, p. 260.

A desperate attack on someone by a bird, from the instigation of the panel is specified in her indictment.   *Ibid.*, p. 271.

Jonet Thomeson testified much displeasure with Andrew Burwick for refusing her some corn, and departed full of wrath. "Quhen the corne was caryit to the grind it lap upoun his wyffis face lyk myttis, and as it war nipit hir face vntill it swallit: and quhen it was maid in meat, he and his wyfe culd not feilt the smell of it: and quhen the eattit of it, it went owre lyk preinis, and culd not be quencit for thirst: and the dogis wold not eat of it—and quhen they chaingit the same with their neighbouris, it was fund sufficient, without any evill taist."   —*Ibid.*, p, 266.

A man suffered various injuries; his cows lost their milk, or cast their calves, and his daughter fell sick during half-a-year; all through the malevolence of Jonet Thomeson; but on his reproving her, "the las becam whole: and having a mear lyk to die, he gave hir almis to heale hir, and the mear was presentlie maid whole."   —*Ibid.*, p. 58.

Being urged "to goe and look vpon" a man who had contract-ed a desperate malady after her imprecations; on her com-pliance, along with some other remedies, he returned to his work on the same day. Also, having quarrelled with another, "his mear took seiknes and was lyk to die; and shoe cuming to the hous, the bairnis gave hir almis to look vpone the mear, she was immediatlie maid quhole."   —*Ibid.*, p. 59.
Trial of Helen Wallas, 1616.—Helen Wallas was indytit for witchcraft chiefly on the following grounds:— "That Wil-liam Holland and she haveing discordit for ane peice of gras,

the said William being keiping his kyne on the said gers sche come to him, and efter mony injurious wordis, raif the curtch aff her heid and pat it vnder hir belt, shuik hir hair about hir [head], and ran to the Ladie Chappell hard by, and went thryse about it vpoun hir bair kneis, prayand cursingis and maledictiounes lycht vpoun for the woman, and cast his left fute shoe over the hous, and gif it fell to the hous1 he wald speid, and gif fra the hous he wald nocht. . . . Item, in that in beir seidtyme a yeir syne, Peter Hollandis wyfe come to the said Helen, the said Peter being seik, and askit at hir quidder or nocht hir husband wald die or leive. The said Helen commandit hir to tak his left fute shoe and cast it ouir the hous, and said gif the mouth of it fell up he wald leive, and gif doun he wald die. Item, for that hir dochter haveing cum to the gudwyfe the said William, and thairefter come to the said William his hous, and zeid sa about his fyir syde, and did the lyk; and thairefter cuming furth quhair his guidis wes pasturing, said thir wordis to thame following:—(Gleib wind luik in the air of the lift, and never have power to eat meat). Swa it fell out that his beastis dwyneit away day lie be hir divilrie. Item, in doing of the lyk to David Wod in Marsetter, ane yeiris syne or thairby. Item, in that Adame Bewis, in, being a young man, and owand hir dochter, sche desyrit him to mak tua corssis, and lay in the watter ane for the man and the vther of Wall, and desyrit sum meall and a drink of milk, quhilk being offerit to hir, sche desyrit that the milk and the meall mycht be baikeit togither, quhilk being done, the gudwyfe of Wall gave hir the half thairof, quhilk she caryit to the said Helen, hir mother, and thairefter the kow that gave the milk lost hir milk, and gave onlie bluid, quhill Hallowmes being half a yeir thairefter." ROGERS, vol. iii. pp. 302, 303.

A cow almost suffocated by falling into the mire, was preserved by three ears of barley spit upon, put into her mouth.
—DALYELL, p. 389.

Trial of Agnes Yulloch or Tulloch, 1616.—Against Agnes Yulloch [or Tulloch] was charged the "abominable cryme of witchcraft, inasmuch that Marjorie Swonay, being chargeit to the toun for sindrie poyntis of witchcraft, sche said to the said Agnes Zullock, gif she come nocht home agane, mak hir to pas that same way, for said she, 'Ye have als guid skill as I.' Item, for that sa lang as James Swoney interteinit hir in his house his cornes and guidis prosperit, bot alsoone as she went out of his hous, he lost baith the profeit of his cornes and guidis be hir divilrie and witchcraft. Item, for that Oliver Faquoy, and Marioun Sclatter, his wyfe, thrie yieris syne or thereby, passing to the hous of Scorne to ane arff, the said Agnes being thair. The guidwyfe of Scorne being seik, the said Marioun Sclatter fand falt for hir being thair. Quha immediatlie tuik seiknes, and thairefter send for the said Agnes, and recoverit hir health be hir divilrie. Item, for that sum evill speiches being betwix Marioun Lincletter, spous to Henrie Growgar in Birsay, and Elspeth Browne, spous to David Mair thair, the said Agnes come to the said Henryes hous, and thair fleat wt. the said Marioun Lincletter, quha immediatlie thairefter contractit seiknes and dyit. The guidwyf of Langskaill, reproveing hir thairof, sche lykwayis fell seik, and lay fourtein dayis, and haveing send for the said Agnes, threattining to dilait hir, the said Agnes tuicheing hir, sche recoverit hir health."
ROGERS, vol. iii. pp. 301, 302.

Stromness. *Bessie Miller,* 1814.—At the village of Stromness, lived, in 1814, an aged dame called Bessie Miller, who helped out her subsistence by telling favourable winds to mariners.

[An account of her is given by Sir W. Scott, who seems to have visited her.]

—SCOTT, The Pirate, note G.

For Witches see also under I. g, I. h, "SEA."

Lightning Source UK Ltd.
Milton Keynes UK
UKOW02f0647271216

290796UK00001BA/30/P